Successful Dinner Parties

ROBERT CARRIER'S KITCHEN

Successful Dinner Parties

Marshall Cavendish   London Sydney & New York

Editor	Grizelda Wiles
Editorial Staff	Carey Denton
	Roz Fishel
	Caroline Macy
	Penny Smith
Art Editor	Ross George
Series Editor	Pepita Aris
Production Executive	Robert Paulley
Production Controller	Steve Roberts

Photography
Bryce Attwell: 42, 64
Theo Bergstrom: 34
Paul Bussell: 2, 38, 92
Laurie Evans: 12, 46
James Jackson: 14, 102
Jhon Kevern: 84
Chris Knaggs: 10, 56, 60, 74
David Levin: 107
Peter Myers: 16, 20, 24, 28, 70, 78, 98
Paul Webster: 52
Paul Williams: 8, 88
Peter Williams: 13
Cover picture: **Theo Bergstrom**

Weights and measures
Both metric and imperial measurements are given. As these are not exact equivalents, please work from one set of figures or the other. Use graded measuring spoons levelled across.

Time symbols
The time needed to prepare the dish is given on each recipe. The symbols are as follows:

 simple to prepare and cook

 straightforward but requires more skill or attention

 time-consuming to prepare or requires extra skill

 must be started 1 day or more ahead

On the cover: Boeuf à la ficelle, Pommes au beurre, Sautéed courgettes and Chocolate fancy cake, page 34

This edition published 1985
© Marshall Cavendish Limited 1984/85

Printed in Italy by
L.E.G.O. S.p.a Vicenza

Typeset by Quadraset Limited, Midsomer Norton, Bath, Avon

Published by Marshall Cavendish House
58 Old Compton Street
London W1V 5PA
ISBN 0 86307 264 X (series)
ISBN 0 86307 398 0 (this volume)

Contents

If you have ever had to give a dinner party but not known what to cook, then this volume is just what you need. *Successful Dinner Parties* is full of complete menus for entertaining guests — ranging from exotic French cuisine to a more simple-to-prepare, but equally delicious, three-course-meal where you can cheat a little with ready-prepared ingredients. I particularly recommend this menu — which has Veal in soured cream as its main course — for those occasions when you want to entertain but at the same time take things easy. You'll also find hints to help you organize the shopping, tips on how best to present the food and comprehensive instructions on how to set and decorate the table to best effect. Each menu has a plan-ahead timetable to enable you to prepare the meal with maximum efficiency, and suggestions for the wine which best complements the dish.

Perhaps, if you would like to entertain in a traditional way, you should try my Pan-fried sirloin with mustard glaze followed by a country-style Adam and Eve pudding served warm with whipped cream. Or, as an alternative, delight your friends with my Mexican-style meal of Seviche or Raw mushroom and prawn appetizer, followed by Chili con carne with plenty of lager to drink. A novel way to end this meal is by letting your guests choose the filling for their Mexican custard tarts from a selection of three different flavours.

For those of you who like to prepare the bulk of the meal well ahead so that you can sit down with a quick aperitif before your guests arrive, I have included a meal with a Mediterranean flavour. The main course is Fried chicken and spinach with a side dish of Potatoes Anna, an usual way of using potatoes by layering them with butter and then baking them in the oven.

I think no book on dinner parties would be complete without a traditional menu for fresh game so I have also included a recipe for Roast grouse with a juicy stuffing of apple, orange and onion. Serve with crispy Game chips, and end the meal with a very English Cheddar or ripe Stilton. And do bear in mind that no matter which of my menus you choose, you can be assured of a successful dinner party and a meal to remember.

Happy cooking and bon appétit!

Robert Carrier

Planning a Dinner Party

SETTING THE SCENE

Planning a dinner party does not stop at selecting the food — laying and decorating the table are just as important to make the evening a really successful and memorable occasion.

For a successful dinner party, creating the right atmosphere is as important as being able to produce well-chosen, beautifully cooked food. This atmosphere is greatly helped by careful planning of the menu, the preparation time and how the table looks.

Planning the menu

First of all decide how many courses you want to include in the meal. Three is quite normal, plus a cheese board. Four courses are reasonable if you are able to manage the cooking. Or, to make serving at the table easier, start with finger food that you offer round with the aperitifs, moving onto a more substantial dish as the first course at the table.

A lot of the cooking should be done ahead; do the least possible while the guests are present. Start by planning the main course. Choose a dish that can be cooked ahead and will not spoil if it has to sit in the oven. Roasts and braises are generally good choices for this reason, although a roast needs to be carved and kept warm. Ready-portioned dishes like a casserole or braise are by far the easiest to serve successfully. For large parties avoid dishes which need a lot of attention at the last moment, for example, a sauté.

To go with the main course, choose one vegetable that, once it is cooked, will keep hot without spoiling — a gratin or roast potatoes, for example. An alternative is to serve a tossed salad with the main course instead of a cooked vegetable.

Selecting a dessert is easy. There are any number of cold prepare-ahead dishes. Another idea is to offer one very light dish and one that is more substantial.

The first course is often the most difficult to decide upon. Remember, it must complement the main course and not deaden the appetite. For ease, choose something cold that can be prepared and served onto individual plates in advance.

As a general rule, when planning your menu, make sure that you take into account the colours and textures of the dishes you are putting together. Also, make sure that the meal is balanced.

Making lists

Having worked out your menu, write down everything needed, then divide up the list. In section one note all the store-cupboard basics to be bought a week ahead. Make a second list of shopping that can be done 3–4 days before, then make a final one of all the food that must be bought at the last moment, such as meat, cream, vegetables and fresh fruit.

Freezer tips

Use your freezer to ease last-minute pressure; cook ahead and freezer certain items that will be useful.

● Pastry keeps well for several weeks in the freezer — make and bake tart cases ahead.
● Some soups and most pâtés freeze well; so this may be the answer to choosing your first course.
● If using, prepare and freeze ahead beef stock, bechamel sauce, sauce espagnole or demi-glace. The sauces you cannot freeze include mayonnaise and any related sauces, and custards.
● An iced dessert is another obvious candidate for the freezer.
● Cakes and the sponges for a gateau or trifle freeze very well too, but don't decorate them. Leave this, and any assembling, for the day of the dinner party.

Laying the table

In the past, many strict dos and don'ts governed formal table settings, but now there is a relaxed attitude about what goes on the table and where. Generally, the bywords to take note of are neatness and common sense.

If you are lucky enough to have a polished table, you will also have heat-resistant mats. If you plan to use a tablecloth, perhaps to disguise an awkward table extension, then white or plain pastel shades are classic. Any tablecloth lies better over a felt undercloth, which gives the table a slightly padded, well-dressed appearance.

In order to help your guests choose correctly through what may be several courses, the cutlery is arranged in order of its use, from the outside working in towards the main plate. Put the knives on the right with blades towards the main plate, and the forks on the left. Because the bread and butter knife is generally the first to be picked up, it is often on the far right, but to save space it may go on the side plate on the left of the forks. Cutlery for the dessert may be laid in advance or can be brought in with the dessert.

Water glasses are usually set with the wine glasses. If you are planning to serve white and red wines, then lay the first glass to be used (white wine glass) above the main course knife, the water glass in a straight line on the left and the red wine closer to the plate, making a triangle.

In these days of paper napkins, guests may appreciate being offered linen ones; white is classic, but you can relate napkins to your overall colour scheme.

The table should be planned so that it looks welcoming but also creates a dramatic effect; precisely how you set and decorate your table will depend on your own equipment, the type of food you choose and your personal taste. Bear in mind that the colours, whether of the food or the table accessories, should complement each other or else contrast.

Presentation is as important as the food

FOLDING NAPKINS

Attractively folded napkins add a touch of sophistication and festivity to your dinner table. It may take you a little time and patience to fold the napkins perfectly, but the end result is well worth the effort.

Try out one of these four patterns following our very easy step-by-step instructions on the right. All the designs can be made with multi-ply paper napkins, which will be labour saving, though the best effects are usually obtained with linen or fabric napkins which have been lightly starched. Depending on the general table settings, napkins can be placed either on the side plate or in the centre of the guest's place. For the Candle use a plain white or a plain coloured napkin and then, if required, a tab of appropriately coloured card with the guest's name written on it can be made and added to the top to simulate the flame.

The Classic fold, made with soft fabric or lightly starched linen, gives a simple but extremely elegant air to any dinner table. The Waterlily, however, may need some careful practice before you produce a perfect flower since the shape is more complicated,

but once the basic folds are mastered, then variations on the theme can be attempted. For instance, the petals can be sharply pointed (see illustration below) or eased out softly (see diagram on the right). Either lightly starched fabric, or large, plain and stiff napkins can be used to produce effective table decorations with this pattern.

The Triangle looks especially pretty if you choose napkins which have fancy borders, though do check that the pattern or colour is the same on both sides of the napkin before you start the folding. This is by far the easiest and quickest design to make but it is also one of the most effective.

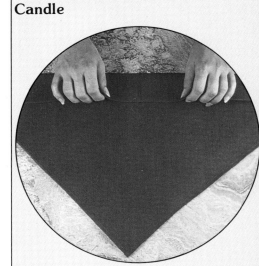

Candle

Fold in half to form a triangle. Turn down the folded edge to make a cuff and press. Turn the napkin over and roll it up.

When folded, tuck the free end of the napkin into the turned-over cuff to hold the finished 'candle' in shape — see left.

Classic fold

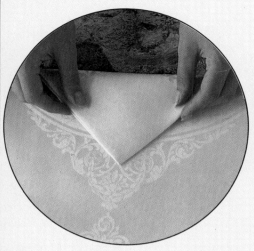  

Fold in 4. Take the point of the folded sides beyond the centre of the square. Press.

Turn the napkin over and fold back the points on either side as shown. Press.

Tuck one flap into the pocket that is formed by the other one.

Waterlily

Fold the four points into the centre to make a smaller square. Repeat this twice more.

Turn the folded napkin over, and fold the four points to meet in the centre.

Hold the centre and pull out 'petals' from the corners, then from between the corners.

Triangle

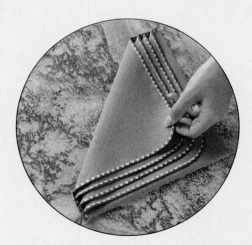

Fold into quarters. Fold back the top point of the unfolded sides as shown.

Fold back the next point to just below the first and repeat with the last two points.

DECORATING THE TABLE

In creating the right atmosphere for your party the table needs to be planned so that it looks welcoming but also creates a dramatic effect; a decorative centrepiece may be the ideal way to add the final touch.

A centrepiece serves as a focal point, drawing together all the table accessories. It may be fruit or flowers, seasonal or classic; it should be low enough to talk across and it should look attractive from a sitting position and from all sides. A rectangular table invites an oval centrepiece, and a round table, a round decoration.

Candles can be pretty and set a very intimate mood. They should be either low or very high; a flame flickering at face level can be irritating to talk across.

Fruit centrepieces
A fruit centrepiece also doubles as dessert, if the guests want to help themselves to fruit with the cheese course, or as a simple alternative to any rich, creamy dessert you may offer them.

Choose fruit in tip-top condition, ripe but not over-ripe, and totally blemish free. Contrasting shapes and colours add to the visual appeal. Purple grapes and yellow bananas make good neighbours, as do black figs and mangoes. Although lemons are not a dessert fruit, they are an invaluable addition for colour. Peaches, nectarines and apricots also look charming grouped together, to emphasize their subtle shades.

A shallow bowl, tray or even a wooden board makes all the fruit visible and accessible; the height can come from the arrangement itself. A trio of solid fruit, such as apples or oranges, makes a good base. Work upwards and outwards, lightest and softest fruits go on last (see picture).

Cocktail sticks or children's modelling paste can be used to secure fruit at a desired angle. A cocktail stick stuck at an angle into an apple or orange can stop it rolling off, while smaller fruit like apricots can be secured in groups of two or three.

Floral arrangements
To allow cross-table conversation, look for a small, fairly shallow container and use some florist's green sponge to help you make a flower arrangement that is stylish and elegant without being bulky. Saturate the block with water before you start. Recut all the stem ends of your flowers and give them a long, deep drink in water before arranging them. As you make the arrangement, check the appearance from sitting height and from different sides.

If you want the colour and perfume of flowers without the complication of a formal arrangement, there are some lovely options. For example, bunches of violets amassed in a long, shallow dish are successful because of their utter simplicity. You can also try a Japanese-style arrangement. A shallow glass dish, perhaps with a mirror in the bottom and a few pebbles or shells, can be filled with water. On top float flattish flowers, such as anemones.

Or try individual arrangements for each guest. A perfect white camellia, floating in a finger bowl at each place setting, or a single rose in a wine glass, are very effective.

An attractive, yet practical, centrepiece

DRINKS FOR DINNER PARTIES

Choose aperitifs, wines and liqueurs that complement the food you are going to serve your guests — careful thought rather than expense is the key to interesting and pleasurable drinking.

Once you have decided upon the food for your dinner party it is time to choose the drinks you will be serving with it. This applies not only to the wine that you drink with the meal, but to any drinks you may be having as aperitifs, as well as after-dinner drinks such as liqueurs or special coffees.

Aperitifs

The purpose of an aperitif — from the Latin *aperire* 'to open' — is to sharpen the appetite and taste buds of your guests, as well as to create a relaxed atmosphere of anticipation for the food to come.

Drinks which are suitable to serve as aperitifs include the fortified wines like Madeira or sherry; either the dry, pale finos or the sweeter, darker amontillados; a chilled white port or a dry white vermouth, served chilled with ice and topped up with soda. Bitters, particularly Campari, served in a similar way, are also popular.

Wine can also be served as an aperitif — something cool, light, dry and white is refreshing and very acceptable. Universally popular is champagne, but the wines of the Loire, Reislings and Chardonnays, Italian Soave and Frascati and Portuguese Vinho Verde are all suitable. A dry rosé is another possibility.

For something more unusual, add some crème de cassis (blackcurrant cordial) to a dry white wine to make Kir, or crème de framboise (raspberry) to still or sparkling wine. Soda with still wine and orange juice with sparkling wine are other suggestions.

Wine

Although it is perfectly possible to drink any wine with any food, it is worth at least considering general guidelines which will help to avoid real disasters and increase the combined enjoyment of food and wine.

Always progress from the lesser wines to the better ones (or the difference will be obvious to all) and remember, lighter, drier wines should come before those that are fuller-bodied and heavier in taste.

Food from a particular region will often match a type of wine from the same region. Bear in mind that if you use a particular wine in the making of a dish, it is likely to be the best one to drink with that dish.

Watch out for foods that are difficult to match. Try to avoid drinking good wine with food that contains vinegar. Acidic fruit, like oranges, lemons and pineapple react badly with wine, as does chocolate.

If you do serve a salad as a side dish, try to keep the dressing light (preferably made with lemon juice rather than vinegar) and serve something bland, such as bread, to act as a barrier between the salad and the wine.

Eggs and egg dishes mask wines so there is no point serving them with one which is

Wines from the southern Rhône valley

fine or delicate. Highly spiced food and curries which are not too hot may be served with fuller-flavoured white wines such as Gewürztraminers, while Chinese food requires only a light, sweetish rosé (Mateus or Rosé d'Anjou) or a Riesling.

With the first course: if you wish to open the meal with a different wine from your main course, try an aromatic, dry white wine. This should stimulate the appetite without being too pungent (which might be difficult to follow).

Alsatian Gewürztraminer and Fumé Blanc from California are very good choices for serving with smoked fish starters; they are also delicious with all sorts of different pâtés. Or try a French Sauvignon, like Sancerre, or one of the many Sauvignons from Central Europe.

A light, dry white wine will go very well with simply cooked fish such as sole, or with pasta and shellfish dishes. Muscadets, Chardonnays from France and California, Vinho Verde, or even a dry, white Rioja are all suitable.

With the main course: there are certain combinations of food and wine that are particularly good.

Poultry and lamb: it is a very good idea to choose clarets to go with not-so-heavy meats like poultry and lamb. More expensive examples from Bordeaux are St Emilion and Pomerol, both blends of Cabernet and Merlot grapes. Cabernet Sauvignon wines from Australia, South Africa or America or a *Gran Reserva* Rioja could all be served to good effect.

Game: serve a full and heavy burgundy

light Loire wine goes well with simply prepared grilled fish. If the fish is served with a sauce, a delicately flavoured wine will be lost. Choose, instead, a fuller flavoured wine, like a white burgundy or the full-bodied white from Robert Mondavi's vineyards in California. Or try a young claret, a Mâcon-Prissé or a Mâcon-Villages.

Salad: as a main course it can be partnered by one of the dry, stronger rosés such as Tavel, a light provençal red wine or a light Italian red wine such as Valpolicella.

With the dessert: dessert wines are becoming more and more popular. They are best served with simple, fruity or light, creamy puddings rather than very rich and creamy sweets. Sauternes and Barsac are the classic French dessert wines, with Château d'Yquem and Château Climens among the most famous of them. Muscat-de-Beaumes-de-Venise from the Côtes-du-Rhône is an excellent choice too. There are many German dessert wines to choose from, as well as Tokay from Hungary. Sweet champagne, sparkling wines such as Asti Spumante, Madeira and cream sherry can all be served.

With the cheeseboard: the traditional French custom of serving cheese before the dessert allows the wine served with the main course to be finished. If you prefer cheese after your dessert, serve it with port.

Once you have made a careful selection of the wine for your dinner party, make sure that you keep it and present it properly. Good red wine needs at least three days to settle after it has been moved around. Uncork all the bottles of red wine you are sure to need at least 2 hours before you plan to serve them, leave them (plus any spares) at room temperature. Chill white wine for two hours in the refrigerator before serving.

Allow a glass each for the first course wine and again for the dessert wine. For the main course you should allow at least 2 glasses of wine per person.

After-dinner drinks
Cognac is a popular choice to follow a dessert wine, but many people choose to drink a sweet liqueur after red wine. A selection of miniature bottles offers an element of choice but if you decide to buy one bottle of liqueur plus cognac, go for an orange-flavoured Grand Marnier or Cointreau.

Coffee
A cup of real, preferably freshly ground, coffee is the perfect end to a meal. For a special dinner, try a special ending with a liqueur coffee topped with cream. Serve in clear, stemmed glasses so you can see the layers. Warm the glasses first by running them under hot water, then dry them thoroughly. The alcohol goes in first, then a little sugar is added. Pour in the hot coffee and stir until the sugar is dissolved. When the coffee is still piping hot, hold a spoon over the glass with its back facing upwards. Carefully pour the cream over the back of the spoon so that it trickles down into the glass and floats on top of the coffee. If you are using lightly whipped cream, spoon it carefully on top of the coffee. In both cases the coffee should be drunk through the layer of cream, without stirring.

with any sort of game. Nuits St Georges and Côte de Beaune are probably the best known burgundies traditionally served with game. Equally suitable are Rhône wines such as Châteauneuf-du-Pape.

Beef: either Burgundy or Bordeaux wines and their many equivalents around the world can be drunk happily with beef. Australian Shiraz wines are excellent, as are burgundies, such as those from the Côte d'Or and Côte Chalonnaise. Italian Chianti Classico and Spanish Riojas such as Marques de Riscal and Marques de Murieta are also good. Try a South African Pinotage from Meerendal in the Cape region.

Pork: if you prepare pork with a rich sauce, choose a powerful wine, such as Hermitage

Liqueur coffees round off that special meal

or Côte Rôtie, to go with it. If the pork is cooked simply, then choose a more delicate wine, such as Pouilly-Fuissé.

Fish and white meat: it is traditional to serve white wine with fish, but this is one of the conventions which can be broken. A light red wine, such as a well-chilled beaujolais or a young red wine from Bordeaux or the Loire, goes extremely well with salmon and trout. One of the better rosés, a Tavel or a Coteaux d'Ancenis from the Loire, will make an excellent accompaniment to fish and lighter meats.

The type of white wine you serve with fish will depend on how the fish is prepared. A

Lamb

LAMB WITH AN ORIENTAL TOUCH

A soufflé starter will always win you compliments, especially if its presentation is original — like my pretty Stuffed tomato soufflés. Some people shy away from soufflés because of the precise timing involved but there is no real difficulty in this instance; just have the mixture ready before your guests arrive, then fold in the beaten egg white at the last minute and cook the tomato cases in the oven while you finish your aperitif. It is a little fiddly to skin the cooked tomatoes, but much nicer to eat if you do. Don't peel off the skins before cooking because the tomato cases will tend to collapse in the oven.

One small point — remember that your guests will cope with waiting for the soufflés a few extra minutes far better than the soufflés will cope with being kept waiting by your guests!

For Chinese lamb with mange tout, choose tender, young, lean lamb and cut it into fine strips, Chinese-style. Serve it with gleaming Two-tone turmeric rice. For this attractive dish, turmeric-yellow rice is mixed with plain white rice to make a dish that is subtly shaded in colour. A simple salad, Cucumber, watercress and onion top panaché, finishes off the main course to perfection.

Almond apricot crêpes are easy to prepare for a party. Make the crêpes (*page 41*) the day before or even earlier; they will keep very well in your refrigerator, stacked and either wrapped in foil or put in an airtight plastic bag. Roll them up with apricot jam and coat them with the delicious soured cream and almond sauce before your guests arrive. Pop them under the grill after the main course and decorate them quickly just before serving.

Stuffed tomato soufflés

—

Chinese lamb with
mange tout

—

Cucumber, watercress
and onion top panaché

—

Two-tone turmeric rice

—

Almond apricot crêpes

Wine: Chinon red

Plan-ahead timetable

On the day before the meal
Almond apricot crêpes: make the crêpes (*page 41*).
Stack them in a plastic bag or foil and refrigerate.

Two hours before the meal
Chinese lamb with mange tout: prepare the lamb strips and the
mange tout. Leave the meat to come to room temperature.
Stuffed tomato soufflés: make the bechamel sauce, reduce;
whisk in egg yolk and cheese. Prepare the tomato cases.
Almond apricot crêpes: fill the crêpes with apricot jam and roll
them up tightly. Prepare the almond, soft brown sugar and
soured cream coating. Grate the orange zest.

One hour before the meal
Cucumber, watercress and onion top panaché: prepare and
assemble the salad. Make the vinaigrette.

Thirty minutes before the meal
Chinese lamb with mange tout: blanch the mange tout.
Two-tone turmeric rice: cook, sauté and keep warm separately.

Twenty minutes before the meal
Stuffed tomato soufflés: whisk the egg white. Fold it into the
sauce. Fill the tomato cases and cook in the oven.

Just before the meal
Stuffed tomato soufflés: skin the tomatoes. Serve.

Between the first and the main course
Chinese lamb with mange tout: season and sauté the lamb.
Finish cooking it and transfer it to a serving dish. Serve.
Two-tone rice: transfer to a serving dish, toss lightly and serve.
Cucumber, watercress and onion top panaché: pour the
vinaigrette over and serve.

Between the main course and the dessert
Almond apricot crêpes: heat through, decorate and serve.

Stuffed tomato soufflés

Serves 4

8 medium-sized firm tomatoes	**For the bechamel sauce**
1 egg, separated	**(makes 175 ml /6 fl oz)**
45 ml /3 tbls freshly grated	20 g /¾ oz butter
Gruyère cheese	15 ml /1 tbls flour
salt and freshly ground black	200 ml /7 fl oz milk
pepper	¼ chicken stock cube
freshly grated nutmeg	½ bay leaf
butter, for greasing	3 white peppercorns
parsley sprigs, to garnish	a good pinch of grated nutmeg

1 Make the bechamel sauce: melt the butter in a small pan over a low
heat and then stir in the flour and cook for 2–3 minutes, stirring
constantly with a wooden spoon.
2 Scald the milk in another pan. Stir one-quarter of the heated milk
into the roux of flour and butter, off the heat. Return it to a low heat
and bring to the boil, stirring vigorously.
3 As the sauce begins to thicken, add the remainder of the milk, a
little at a time, stirring briskly between additions. Continue stirring
until the sauce bubbles, and is therefore cooked.
4 Add the crumbled stock cube, bay leaf, peppercorns and nutmeg.
The sauce must now infuse and reduce in quantity to 175 ml /6 fl oz.
An easy way to see when the sauce has reduced to exactly this quantity
is to pour it into a boil-proof measuring jug. Stand this in a pan of
gently bubbling water and simmer gently, stirring from time to time,
until the sauce is exactly 175 g /6 fl oz.
5 Meanwhile, cut the stalk end off each tomato, a quarter of the way
down, and discard them. Using a sharp teaspoon or a grapefruit knife,
remove the central core and seeds and discard. Turn the prepared
tomatoes upside down and leave them to drain.
6 Whisk the egg yolk and the Gruyère cheese into the sauce. Season
to taste with salt, pepper and nutmeg. Reserve until needed.
7 Heat the oven to 220C /425F /gas 7.
8 In a clean, dry bowl, whisk the egg white with a pinch of salt until
soft peaks form. Fold this into the sauce with a metal spoon.
9 Grease a shallow ovenproof dish. Place the drained tomatoes in the
prepared dish and carefully spoon the mixture into the cavities. Bake in
the oven for 10–12 minutes, or until the soufflés have risen and are
golden brown.
10 Transfer the tomatoes to individual serving dishes, peeling off the
skins, which will be split and loose, and garnish each serving with
parsley sprigs. Serve immediately.

 1¼ hours

Chinese lamb with mange tout

Serves 4
700 g /1½ lb lean lamb slices, 5mm /¼ in thick, cut from the fillet
end of the leg
freshly ground black pepper
225 g /8 oz mange tout, topped and tailed
salt
30 ml /2 tbls olive oil
60 ml /4 tbls chicken stock, home-made or from a cube
30 ml /2 tbls soy sauce
5 ml /1 tbls soft brown sugar
5 ml /1 tsp cornflour

1 Slice the lamb across the grain into thin strips, about 10 mm /½ in wide and 7.5 cm /3 in long. Season generously with freshly ground black pepper and bring to room temperature.
2 Diagonally slice each mange tout across into 3 pieces. Bring a saucepan of salted water to the boil and blanch the mange tout for 2 minutes, then drain well.
3 Heat the olive oil in a large frying-pan or wok. Season the lamb with salt to taste. When the oil is sizzling, sauté the lamb strips for about 4 minutes, or until they are golden, over a high heat, tossing them constantly with a spatula.
4 Add the chicken stock and soy sauce to the lamb. Stir in the soft brown sugar and simmer gently for 2 minutes. Add the blanched mange tout and then continue to simmer for 2 minutes.
5 In a small bowl, blend the cornflour with a little of the lamb juices to make a smooth paste, then pour most of the remaining lamb juices onto the blended cornflour, stir to blend and return it to the frying-pan or wok. Simmer for about 1 minute, or until the sauce has thickened and has the consistency of a glaze. Season with freshly ground black pepper to taste and transfer to a heated serving dish. Serve immediately.

 bringing the meat to room temperature,
then 30 minutes

 a Chinon red

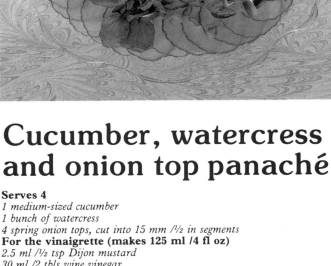

Cucumber, watercress and onion top panaché

Serves 4
1 medium-sized cucumber
1 bunch of watercress
4 spring onion tops, cut into 15 mm /½ in segments
For the vinaigrette (makes 125 ml /4 fl oz)
2.5 ml /½ tsp Dijon mustard
30 ml /2 tbls wine vinegar
salt and freshly ground black pepper
90 ml /6 tbls olive oil

1 Wipe the cucumber with a damp cloth, then slice it into thin rounds. Arrange it in a shallow serving dish, layering up the slices in neat, overlapping rows.
2 Wash the watercress in several changes of cold water and remove any yellow or damaged leaves. Drain and dry it well with a clean tea-towel or absorbent paper. Remove and discard the stems.
3 Arrange clusters of watercress over the cucumber, pushing the stem ends between the slices so that the watercress stands up.
4 Sprinkle with spring onion segments.
5 Put the mustard into the bottom of a small jug or cup and add the wine vinegar, the salt, pepper and olive oil. Beat the mixture vigorously with a fork or a whisk to make an emulsion.
6 Pour the dressing over the salad and serve immediately.

 30 minutes

Two-tone turmeric rice

Serves 4
250 g /9 oz long-grain rice
salt
75 g /3 oz butter
7.5 ml /1½ tsp turmeric
freshly ground black pepper

1   Bring a large saucepan of salted water to the boil. Dribble the rice into it, then bring the water back to the boil. Stir once with a wooden spoon to dislodge any grains of rice stuck to the bottom or sides of the pan and cook gently for 18 minutes, or until the rice is barely tender but not mushy. Drain, rinse under cold running water and then drain the rice again.
2   Using 2 medium-sized frying-pans, heat half the butter in each. Add the turmeric to one pan, stirring to blend with a wooden spoon.
3   Add ⅓ of the rice to the turmeric butter and the remaining rice to the second pan. Toss both pans over a moderate heat for 2 minutes, or until the rice is heated through. Season to taste with salt and freshly ground black pepper.
4   Transfer the turmeric rice to a heated serving dish and spoon the plain rice on top.
5   Using a fork, gently and carefully toss the rice together, being careful not to over-work, or the two-tone effect will be lost. Serve immediately.

●   Divide the butter equally between the pans, although the rice is not equally divided. The extra butter is needed to distribute the turmeric colour thoroughly.

 30 minutes

Almond apricot crêpes

Serves 4
8 × 15 cm /6 in French crêpes (page 41)
40 ml /8 tsp apricot jam
60 g /2 oz chopped, blanched almonds
30 ml /2 tbls soft, dark brown sugar
150 ml /5 fl oz soured cream
grated zest of 1 orange
For the decoration
4 fresh apricots

1   Lay the crêpes on a flat surface and spread each one evenly with 5 ml /1 tsp apricot jam. Roll them up tightly and lay them side by side in a flameproof serving dish, leaving a gap between each crêpe.
2   Prepare the decoration: bring a large saucepan of water to the boil and blanch the apricots for 2 minutes. Drain, rinse them under cold running water and drain again. Remove the skins with a sharp knife. Slice each apricot in half and remove the stones.
3   Heat the grill to high.
4   In a bowl, combine the chopped blanched almonds, soft, dark brown sugar and soured cream, stirring until well blended. Spoon the mixture over the middle section of each crêpe to coat.
5   Sprinkle the coated crêpes with the grated orange zest and place under the grill. Grill 7.5 cm /3 in from the heat for 3–4 minutes, or until the crêpes are heated through and the soured cream mixture is tinged with brown.
6   Arrange the prepared halved apricots around the edge of the dish, cut sides down, and serve immediately.

●   If fresh apricots are unavailable, use well-drained canned apricots instead.

 making the crêpes, then 25 minutes

A MENU FROM FRANCE

The French really know how to enjoy good food and wine; bring the flavour of France to your dinner table with this delicious meal for four. Mussels are an inexpensive luxury and these versatile molluscs can be served in a variety of ways. The Mussel salad I have chosen to start this menu is a lightly dressed salad of cold mussels that have been cooked in white wine with shallots and fresh herbs. The dressing is made of the delicious cooking liquor, olive oil and wine vinegar. A word of advice — buy your mussels on the day you intend to eat them.

Whether they are *navarins* or *ragoûts*, the French love stews. Try my favourite variation on the traditional recipe which is usually made with mutton — Navarin of lamb. Slowly stewed in stock and tomato purée, with button onions, potatoes and peas added to the stew to serve, the lamb is tender and aromatic. A green salad is all the accompaniment

needed for this substantial dish. The gentle bite of curly endive with mustard and cress in a dressing of egg vinaigrette quietly offsets any richness in the lamb. To drink with this meal I have chosen a dry red Bourgueil from the Loire region of France.

Both the starter and the main course require very little last-minute attention and no precise timing, leaving you free to concentrate on the Lemon soufflé tart. This light, fluffy mixture baked in a crisp pastry shell is best served hot from the oven.

This sparkling dinner menu brings you all that is best in French cooking — so invite your friends round and enjoy it with them.

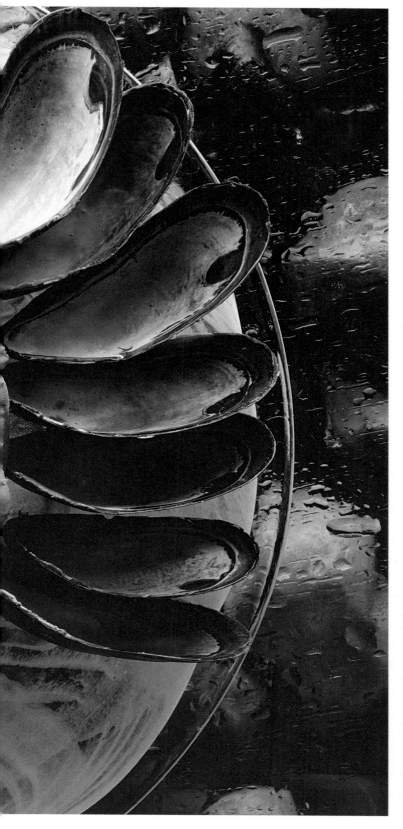

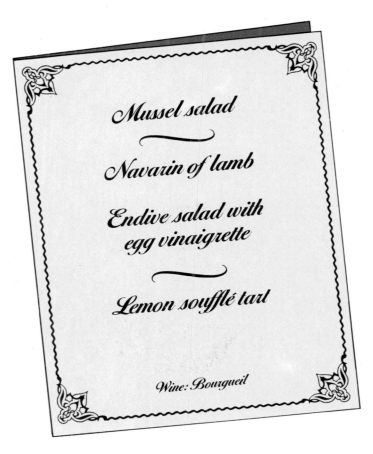

Mussel salad

Navarin of lamb

Endive salad with egg vinaigrette

Lemon soufflé tart

Wine: Bourgueil

Plan-ahead timetable

Three hours before the meal
Lemon soufflé tart: roll out the pastry, prepare the case and chill.
Mussel salad: prepare and cook the mussels, discarding any that do not open. Leave them to get cold.
Navarin of lamb: prepare the meat, sauce and vegetables, and cook in the oven.

Two hours before the meal
Lemon soufflé tart: half-bake the pastry case.

One hour before the meal
Navarin of lamb: sauté the button onions and bacon.

Fifty minutes before the meal
Navarin of lamb: strain the sauce and return it to the oven with the onions, bacon and potatoes.
Endive salad with egg vinaigrette: prepare the endive and the mustard and cress. Make the egg vinaigrette.

Twenty minutes before the meal
Mussel salad: make the dressing.
Lemon soufflé tart: prepare the egg yolk and egg white mixtures, but do not combine.

Just before the meal
Navarin of lamb: add the peas and return to the oven.
Mussel salad: dress the mussels, garnish and serve.

Between the first and the main course
Lemon soufflé tart: combine the egg yolk and white mixtures, fill the case, then bake.
Navarin of lamb: check the seasoning, sprinkle with parsley, garlic and lemon zest and serve.
Endive salad with egg vinaigrette: assemble the salad, dress and serve.

Mussel salad

Serves 4

1 kg /2 lb or 2 pt medium-sized mussels
30 ml /2 tbls finely chopped shallots
2 sprigs of thyme
2 sprigs of parsley
1 bay leaf
150 ml /5 fl oz dry white wine
60 ml /4 tbls finely chopped fresh parsley
buttered brown bread or French bread, to serve

For the dressing

90 ml /6 tbls olive oil
30 ml /2 tbls wine vinegar
salt and freshly ground black pepper

1 Scrub the mussels thoroughly in several changes of cold water and trim off the hairy beards. Discard any cracked mussels or any that have not closed by the end of this operation.

2 Place the prepared mussels in a saucepan with the finely chopped shallots, sprigs of thyme and parsley, bay leaf and white wine. Cover tightly and simmer for 5–7 minutes, or until the mussels open. Reserving the liquid, remove the mussels from the pan with a slotted spoon. (Discard any that have not opened.) Remove the mussels from their shells and transfer them to a serving dish. Keep a few half shells to garnish, if wished. Leave the mussels to cool completely.

3 Meanwhile, prepare the dressing. Strain 75 ml /3 fl oz of the mussel liquid through a muslin-lined sieve into a bowl. Add the olive oil and wine vinegar. Season with salt and freshly ground black pepper to taste. Beat with a fork until the mixture emulsifies.

4 Pour the emulsified dressing over the cold mussels. They should be moist, but without excess dressing. Garnish the dish with a few reserved half shells, if wished. Sprinkle the mussels with finely chopped parsley and serve immediately, with buttered brown bread or French bread.

30 minutes, plus cooling

Navarin of lamb

Serves 4

1.4 kg /3 lb boned shoulder of lamb
(1.8 kg /4 lb before boning)
salt
freshly ground black pepper
40 g /1½ oz butter
45 ml /3 tbls olive oil
1 Spanish onion, quartered
a pinch of sugar
30 ml /2 tbls flour
425 ml /15 fl oz beef stock,
*   home-made or from a cube*
45 ml /3 tbls tomato purée

2 turnips, quartered
bouquet garni
8 button onions
100 g /4 oz unsmoked bacon,
*   diced*
8 small potatoes
100 g /4 oz frozen peas
30 ml /2 tbls finely chopped
*   fresh parsley*
1 small garlic clove, finely
*   chopped*
grated zest of 1 lemon

1 Heat the oven to 180C /350F /gas 4. Cut the lamb into 4 cm /1½ in cubes, discarding most fat and all the gristle. Season generously.

2 Heat 25 g /1 oz butter and 30 ml /2 tbls olive oil in a flameproof casserole. Brown the meat on all sides, in 4 batches, transferring each browned batch to a plate with a slotted spoon. Keep warm.

3 Add the quartered Spanish onion to the casserole. Sprinkle with a pinch of sugar and brown on all sides. Stir in the flour and cook over a low heat for 3 minutes to make a pale roux. Pour in the beef stock, stir vigorously and bring to the boil. Stir in the tomato purée and blend well. Add the quartered turnips and the bouquet garni and return the browned meat to the pan. Season to taste, then cover and cook in the oven for 1½ hours.

4 Meanwhile, in a small frying-pan, melt the remaining butter and olive oil. When the foaming subsides, add the button onions. Toss over a moderate heat for 5–7 minutes, or until golden brown. Remove with a slotted spoon to a plate and keep warm. Sauté the diced bacon in the remaining fat for 4 minutes, or until golden. Add to the browned onions and keep warm.

5 Remove the lamb from the casserole and keep warm. Strain the sauce and discard the vegetables and bouquet garni; return the sauce to the casserole. Skim off any fat, then return the lamb to the casserole with the sautéed onions, bacon and the potatoes. Cover and return the casserole to the oven. Cook for 40 minutes.

6 Remove the lid and stir in the peas. Cook for a further 10 minutes, or until the meat and all the vegetables are tender.

7 Adjust the seasoning and sprinkle with finely chopped parsley and garlic and grated lemon zest. Serve very hot from the casserole.

2¾ hours   *Bourgueil*

Endive salad with egg vinaigrette

Serves 4
1 small head of curly endive
1 box of mustard and cress
For the egg vinaigrette
1 egg
2.5 ml /½ tsp Dijon mustard
30 ml /2 tbls wine vinegar
salt and freshly ground black pepper
90 ml /6 tbls olive oil
15 ml /1 tbls finely snipped chives

1   Break the endive into separate leaves. Wash the leaves thoroughly in several changes of cold water and dry them well with a clean tea-towel.
2   Cut the mustard and cress from the box by snipping through the stalks half-way down (discard the bottom half). Wash the top well and keep it in a damp tea-towel until needed.
3   For the egg vinaigrette, first soft boil the egg. Bring a saucepan of water to the boil. Using a spoon, slip the egg into the boiling water. Lower the heat and simmer for 3½ minutes. Remove the egg from the water and place it in cold water to cool completely.
4   Put the mustard in a small cup and add the wine vinegar. Season to taste with salt and freshly ground black pepper. Add the olive oil. Shell the cold egg.
5   Carefully separate the soft-boiled yolk from the white and beat the yolk into the dressing with a fork or whisk until it emulsifies.
6   Chop the egg white finely and add to the vinaigrette with the snipped chives.
7   In a salad bowl, combine the endive with the mustard and cress and toss to mix. Pour the dressing over and toss again until the salad is well coated. Serve immediately.

20 minutes

Lemon soufflé tart

Serves 4
350 g /12 oz made-weight shortcrust pastry, defrosted if frozen
butter, for greasing
1 medium-sized egg white, beaten
4 eggs, separated
175 g /6 oz caster sugar
60 ml /4 tbls lemon juice
a pinch of freshly grated nutmeg
5 ml /1 tsp grated lemon zest
5 ml /1 tsp vanilla essence
salt

1   Roll out the pastry 3–6 mm /⅛–¼ in thick. Lift it onto the rolling pin over a greased 23 cm /9 in flan tin.
2   Press the pastry into the tin from the centre outwards and then fit the sides. Do not stretch it or it will shrink back later. Trim away any extra pastry by rolling over the top of the tin with the pin. (Discard or use in another recipe.) Prick the base with a fork and chill for ½ hour.
3   Heat the oven and a baking sheet to 200C /400F /gas 6. Line the pastry with foil and beans and bake for 10 minutes on the sheet.
4   Turn down the oven to 180C /350F /gas 4. Remove the foil and beans and bake for a further 8–10 minutes.
5   Remove from the oven and brush with egg white to seal. Turn the oven down to 170C /325F /gas 3.
6   In the top pan of a double boiler, beat together with a wooden spoon the egg yolks, 100 g /4 oz caster sugar, the lemon juice and freshly grated nutmeg. Cook over simmering water, beating constantly, for about 10 minutes, or until the mixture has thickened and coats the back of the spoon. Stir in the grated lemon zest and the vanilla essence. Transfer to a large bowl.
7   In a clean, dry bowl, whisk the egg whites with a pinch of salt until they are stiff but not dry. Whisk in the remaining caster sugar, 15 ml / 1 tbls at a time, and whisk until glossy.
8   With a large metal spoon, fold the whisked egg white and sugar mixture into the warm yolk and lemon mixture. Spoon it into the prepared pastry case, easing the mixture right to the sides with a palette knife.
9   Bake immediately for about 30 minutes, or until puffed and golden, then serve.

 1¾ hours, including resting

FOOD LOVERS' DELIGHT

ere is an elegant dinner party menu for four — it needs to be planned with care and attention but the reward is a sophisticated dinner that needs little last-minute fuss. Another pleasing aspect is that it uses ingredients in an unusual way. For instance, we are probably most used to scampi crumbed and deep-fried or served in a sauce such as a Provençal tomato one. Here they are served with sliced new potatoes and marinated in dry white wine, black olives, garlic and herbs.

The main course, Rack of lamb in pastry with walnuts, is another variation on a more familiar theme. Everyone enjoys tender, juicy rack of lamb but serving it with mushroom, ham and walnut stuffing makes it extra special. Finishing touches should never be ignored and it is worth a little extra trouble to buy some cutlet frills and decorate your pastry-wrapped rack in true 'French style'.

Carrot and broccoli towers make a colourful and elegant vegetable accompaniment to the main dish. As they can be prepared in advance, just cooked through and then kept warm in the oven before serving, they are also ideal for any complicated menu that calls for a lot of other last-minute preparation.

The dessert I have chosen to finish this gourmet meal is a delicious variation on the classic Baked Alaska. Tender baked apple containers are filled with raspberries and topped with ice cream and meringue before being quickly baked to make the delicious dessert I have called Baked apple Alaska.

This will be a dinner party that you will remember and enjoy; it combines the two basic principles of pleasurable entertaining — an attractive meal that is a delight to eat, and a relaxed hostess.

Chablis scampi bowl

Rack of lamb in pastry with walnuts

Carrot and broccoli towers

Baked apple Alaska

Wine: Côtes de Bourg or another red bordeaux

Plan-ahead timetable

On the morning of the meal
Rack of lamb in pastry with walnuts: roast the rack of lamb and leave it to become cold. Cook the finely chopped onion in the butter and olive oil. Add the mushrooms, then the chopped ham and walnuts. Leave to become cold.
Chablis scampi bowl: cook the scampi, mix with the lemon juice, salt and cayenne pepper and chill. Cook, peel and slice the potatoes and marinate in the refrigerator.
Baked apple Alaska: prepare and bake the apples in the wine until they are tender, then drain and leave until completely cold. Fill the centres with raspberries and reserve in the refrigerator until they are needed.

Four hours before the meal
Rack of lamb in pastry with walnuts: remove the puff pastry from the freezer.

Three hours before the meal
Carrot and broccoli towers: prepare the carrot purée and spoon the mixture into 4 dariole moulds. Prepare the broccoli purée and spoon the mixture into 4 dariole moulds. Refrigerate the filled moulds until required.

Two hours before the meal
Rack of lamb in pastry with walnuts: press the cold walnut mixture onto the rack. Roll out the defrosted pastry into a rectangle and wrap it around the rack, seal the pastry edges at the bones. Refrigerate until needed.

One hour before the meal
Chablis scampi bowl: drain off and discard the marinade and combine the potatoes with the scampi. Make the dressing and mix it into the salad, then chill the salad in the refrigerator.
Carrot and broccoli towers: remove from the refrigerator.
Rack of lamb in pastry with walnuts: remove from the refrigerator.
Heat the oven to 180C /350F /gas 4.

Thirty minutes before the meal
Carrot and broccoli towers: put the carrot moulds in a roasting pan with boiling water and cook in the oven.

Twenty minutes before the meal
Carrot and broccoli towers: add the broccoli moulds to the carrot moulds in the roasting pan.

Just before the meal
Rack of lamb in pastry with walnuts: turn up the oven to 230C / 450F /gas 8 and cook the rack in the oven during the first course. (After 10 minutes of cooking you will have to remove the foil covering the pastry.)
Carrot and broccoli towers: remove the pan from the oven, add a little hot water to the pan and set over the lowest heat to keep the moulds warm.
Chablis scampi bowl: garnish with hard-boiled egg and fennel.

Between the first and the main course
Rack of lamb in pastry with walnuts: remove from the oven, discard the foil covering the bones, add cutlet frills if wished, place on a serving dish and garnish.
Carrots and broccoli towers: unmould and garnish with finely chopped parsley and sprigs of watercress.

Between the main course and the dessert
Baked apple Alaska: whisk up the egg whites and whisk in the sugar and vanilla essence. Quickly assemble the apple, ice cream and meringue, bake for 4–5 minutes, then serve.

Chablis scampi bowl

Serves 4
250 g /8 oz frozen scampi, defrosted
salt
juice of ½ lemon
cayenne pepper
450 g /1 lb small new potatoes, cooked
4 hard-boiled eggs, sliced
6–8 fennel sprigs
For the marinade
12 black olives, stoned and sliced
90 ml /6 tbls Chablis or another dry white wine
2 shallots, finely chopped
30 ml /2 tbls finely chopped fresh parsley
salt and freshly ground black pepper
1 garlic clove, finely chopped
For the dressing
60 ml /4 tbls olive oil
juice of 1 lemon
salt and freshly ground black pepper
15 ml /1 tbls finely chopped fresh fennel or tarragon

1 Put the scampi into a pan of boiling salted water. Bring back to the boil and simmer for 5 minutes. Drain and leave to cool.
2 In a bowl, combine the scampi with the lemon juice and salt and cayenne pepper to taste. Chill.
3 Peel and slice the new potatoes. Mix together the marinade ingredients in a bowl and add the sliced potatoes. Mix gently, then chill and marinate for at least 1 hour.
4 One hour before serving, drain off the marinade liquids and transfer the potato slices to a dark-coloured serving dish. Add the scampi and toss well.
5 To make the dressing, beat the olive oil with the lemon juice and season to taste with salt, freshly ground black pepper and finely chopped fennel or tarragon. Mix the dressing into the salad. Chill.
6 Just before serving, garnish the salad with a ring of hard-boiled egg slices and fennel sprigs.

40 minutes, then chilling,
then 10 minutes assembling

Rack of lamb in pastry with walnuts

Serves 4
1 best end of neck of lamb with 8 cutlets
salt
freshly ground black pepper
25 g /1 oz butter, softened
½ Spanish onion, finely chopped
20 g /¾ oz butter
22 ml /1½ tbls olive oil
100 g /4 oz mushrooms, finely chopped
1 slice of ham, finely chopped
50 g /2 oz walnuts, chopped
400 g /14 oz frozen puff pastry
1 egg, beaten
tomato wedges and parsley, to garnish

1 Ask your butcher to trim off the fat from the rack of lamb, to chine the bone and trim away the top half of each cutlet bone. Heat the oven to 190C /375F /gas 5.
2 Season the lamb generously with salt and freshly ground black pepper, then brush with 15 g /½ oz softened butter. Place the rack in a roasting pan, so that it is supported by its bones, and roast for 20 minutes, or longer if you prefer it well cooked. Allow to go cold.
3 Meanwhile, sauté the onion in the butter and olive oil until the onion is transparent. Add the mushrooms and continue to cook, allowing the juices to run from the mushrooms. Cook for about 30 minutes, stirring frequently, until the mixture is almost dry. Add the chopped ham and walnuts. Season and cook for 1 minute longer. Allow the mixture to become completely cold.
4 Remove the pastry from the freezer about 2 hours before using.
5 Press the chopped onion, mushroom, ham and walnut mixture firmly onto the base and back of the cold meat. Brush with the remaining softened butter. Heat the oven to 230C /450F /gas 8.
6 Roll out the puff pastry and encase the lamb, bringing the short ends of the pastry up to join at the bones. Brush the edges with beaten egg and pinch to seal the pastry. Make 2–3 attractive holes in the pastry, about 20 mm /¾ in across.
7 Decorate the pastry with leaves and tassels cut from any spare trimmings, fixing them on with a little beaten egg. Brush the pastry with egg and cover the exposed bones loosely with a little foil. Place a slightly crumpled piece of foil over the leaves and tassels.
8 Place the lamb on a baking sheet and bake for 10 minutes, then remove the foil covering the decorations and return the lamb to the oven for 10 minutes. Remove the foil, put a paper cutlet frill on each exposed bone, garnish and serve.

30 minutes plus cooling,
then 50 minutes

 Côtes de Bourg or another red bordeaux

Carrot and broccoli towers

Serves 4

50 g /2 oz butter, for greasing
  the dariole moulds
15 ml /1 tbls finely chopped
  parsley, for garnishing
watercress, to garnish
For the carrot towers
450 g /1 lb carrots, diced
25 g /1 oz butter
60 ml /4 tbls chicken stock,
  home-made or from a cube

2 eggs
25 g /1 oz butter, softened
salt and ground black pepper
For the broccoli towers
450 g /1 lb frozen broccoli
40 g /1½ oz butter
60 ml /4 tbls chicken stock
salt and ground black pepper
3 eggs
15 g /½ oz butter, softened

1   Heat the oven to 180C /350F /gas 4. Butter 8 dariole moulds with 50 g /2 oz butter.
To make the carrot towers: place the diced carrots in a saucepan. Cover with cold water, bring to the boil over a high heat, then drain thoroughly.
2   In a clean pan, simmer the blanched carrots in 25 g /1 oz butter, the chicken stock and salt to taste, for about 30 minutes, until the carrots have absorbed most of the liquid and are tender. Be careful not to let the carrots burn.
3   Purée the carrot mixture in a blender, adding the eggs. Transfer the purée to a bowl and stir in the softened butter. Season with salt and freshly ground black pepper to taste. Spoon the mixture into 4 dariole moulds and stand the moulds in a roasting tin. Add enough boiling water to come halfway up the moulds. Cook in the oven for 30 minutes until set.
To make the broccoli towers: place the broccoli in a saucepan, cover with cold water and bring to the boil. Drain and slice thickly.
2   Simmer the blanched broccoli in 40 g /1½ oz butter, the chicken stock and salt to taste, for 20 minutes, until the broccoli has absorbed the liquid and is quite tender. Do not let the broccoli burn.
3   Purée the broccoli mixture in a blender, adding the eggs, then transfer to a bowl and stir in the softened butter. Season with salt and pepper to taste. Spoon the mixture into 4 dariole moulds. Stand the moulds in a roasting tin and add enough boiling water to come halfway up the moulds. Cook in the oven for 20 minutes, or until set.
4   When ready to serve, turn the moulds out and sprinkle with parsley and garnish with watercress.

1¼ hours for the carrot moulds,
1 hour for the broccoli moulds

Baked apple Alaska

Serves 4
2 cooking apples each weighing 250 g /8 oz
150 ml /5 fl oz dry white wine
175–250 g /6–8 oz fresh or frozen raspberries, just defrosted
5 egg whites
275 g /10 oz caster sugar
a few drops vanilla essence
475 ml /17 fl oz vanilla ice cream

1   Heat the oven to 180C /350F /gas 4. Peel and core the apples, making large holes in the centres. Arrange them side by side in a baking dish and pour over the wine. Cover the dish tightly with foil and bake for 1 hour, or until the apples are tender but not disintegrating. Turn the apples over 3 or 4 times while they are baking, so that they absorb the wine evenly in the bottom of the dish.
2   When the apples are cooked, drain them. Allow the apples to become completely cold.
3   Cut the apples in half horizontally and place them, cut-side up, in 4 individual 7.5 cm /3 in gratin dishes. Fill the centre of each halved apple with raspberries and chill for at least 30 minutes.
4   Heat the oven to 240C /475F /gas 9. Whisk the egg whites until they form stiff peaks. Whisk in the caster sugar, 30 ml /2 tbls at a time, and continue to whisk vigorously to form stiff peaks. Flavour with a few drops of vanilla essence. When you come to use the whisked egg white, you can either pipe or spoon it over the apples. If piping, spoon the egg white into a piping bag fitted with a large fluted nozzle ready to use. If spooning, set the egg white aside in a bowl.
5   Remove the apples from the refrigerator and, working quickly, mound the top with ice cream as if to re-shape the apples. Pipe or spoon meringue in a spiral around and over each apple to cover it completely.
6   Bake the apples for 4–5 minutes, just long enough to set the surface of the meringue and tinge it with brown. Serve at once.

1¼ hours plus chilling,
then 25 minutes

SUMMER CELEBRATION

Plan-ahead timetable

On the day before the meal
Strawberry water-ice with Grand Marnier: make the water-ice and freeze.
Cigarettes russes: make the Cigarettes russes, cool and store in an airtight tin.

On the morning of the meal
Crab ramekins: prepare the mixture. Fill the ramekins and cover with cling film until needed.

Two hours before the meal
Braised chicory with orange: prepare the chicory, orange zest and juice, assemble the dish and transfer it to the oven.
Medallions of lamb with mint: prepare the lamb rolls and sauté them. Cut the rolls into medallions. Make the quick meat glaze.

One hour before the meal
Courgette purée in potato baskets: peel and dice the courgettes. Salt and leave to stand. Peel, slice and julienne the potatoes. Keep in water until needed.
Gratin dauphinois. prepare and assemble the gratin and transfer it to the oven.

Forty-five minutes before the meal
Courgette purée in potato baskets: cook and purée the courgettes; keep warm. Drain and dry the potatoes, prepare and deep fry the julienne potato baskets and keep warm.

Ten minutes before the meal
Crab ramekins: sprinkle with breadcrumbs and melted butter, cook in the oven, then serve.
Strawberry water-ice with Grand Marnier: transfer to the main part of the refrigerator.

Between the first and the main course
Medallions of lamb with mint: cook the medallions and transfer to a serving dish. Make the sauce, pour it over the medallions, garnish and serve.
Courgette purée in potato baskets: put the purée in the baskets. Transfer to a plate, garnish and serve.
Braised chicory with orange: serve straight from the oven.
Gratin dauphinois: serve straight from the oven.

Between the main course and the dessert
Strawberry water-ice with Grand Marnier and Cigarettes russes: put scoops of water-ice in glass dishes, decorate with halved strawberries and serve with Cigarettes russes.

Crab ramekins

*Medallions of lamb
with mint*

*Courgette purée in
potato baskets*

Gratin dauphinois

Braised chicory with orange

*Strawberry water-ice
with Grand Marnier*

Cigarettes russes

Wine: *Château Palmer*

Crab ramekins

Serves 4
350 g /12 oz crabmeat, defrosted if frozen
4 slices white bread, crusts removed
215 ml /7½ fl oz thick cream
4 ml /¾ tsp mustard powder
salt and freshly ground black pepper
5 ml /1 tsp Worcestershire sauce
90 ml /6 tbls fresh white breadcrumbs
30 ml /2 tbls melted butter

1 Heat the oven to 190C /375F /gas 5.
2 If using fresh crabmeat, remove all the bits of cartilage and shell from the meat. Place all the crabmeat, brown and white together, in a bowl.
3 Dice the bread and reserve.
4 In another bowl, combine the thick cream and mustard powder and season to taste with salt and freshly ground black pepper. Stir in the Worcestershire sauce and then the diced bread. Gently fold in the crabmeat, then adjust the seasoning if necessary.
5 Spoon the crabmeat mixture into 4 individual 150 ml /5 fl oz ramekins or soufflé dishes and sprinkle each one evenly with some fresh white breadcrumbs and melted butter. Put in the oven and bake for 10 minutes, or until golden. Serve immediately.

For a delicious start to an elegant dinner party I have chosen Crab ramekins. Fresh, juicy crabmeat is blended with thick cream and seasoned with mustard and Worcestershire sauce. For the busy hostess or host Crab ramekins have a great advantage — they can be prepared well ahead and all you need to do at the last minute is pop them into the oven.

Rich and tasty, it is the perfect appetizer to the delicate main course of gently sautéed Medallions of lamb with mint — *à la nouvelle cuisine*. In a sauce flavoured with lemon juice and fresh mint, the tiny nuggets of lamb should be crisp and brown on the outside but still pink in the centre, full of juices and flavour. Like the crab starter, this dish only needs finishing at the last minute.

Serve the lamb medallions with a creamy Gratin dauphinois, Braised chicory with orange and Courgette purée in potato baskets. The deep-fried potato baskets are crisp and golden, and a good contrast to the smooth, subtle filling. They can be a little tricky to prepare; I suggest you have a practice run ahead of your party! The end result will be worth the effort, and you will feel more confident and relaxed at the last minute. The Gratin dauphinois and the Braised chicory with orange are both dishes which can be prepared in advance so this will leave you free to deal with trickier preparations like the potato baskets.

To finish, serve my Strawberry water-ice with Grand Marnier. The unique character of Grand Marnier somehow brings out the strawberry flavour to the maximum, and the ice has a wonderful smooth and melting texture. Decorate each portion with pretty halved strawberries and spoil your guests further by passing round the classic Cigarettes russes. I must confess that these crisp, little rolled vanilla biscuits are slow and tricky to make, but they can be prepared the day before, so there need be no last minute panic!

To complement your meal, drink a Château Palmer. One of the great wines of Margaux, this wonderful claret has a ravishing bouquet and is full bodied but very light and silky at the same time — the perfect partner to the delicate lamb medallions, which are the main feature of this easy to organize summer menu.

 30 minutes

Medallions of lamb with mint

Serves 4
1½ best ends of neck of lamb (8 cutlets), boned
salt and freshly ground black pepper
75 g /3 oz butter
60 ml /4 tbls olive oil
15 ml /1 tbls lemon juice
30 ml /2 tbls freshly chopped mint
mint leaves, to garnish
For the quick meat glaze
425 g /15 oz good quality canned consommé

1 First make the quick meat glaze: boil the consommé fast for about 25 minutes until it is reduced to 30 ml /2 tbls, then reserve.
2 Prepare the medallions. With a sharp knife, strip off all the fat from the meat so that you are left with just the eye of the meat. Tie at regular intervals with string, then neaten the rolls. Season with salt and freshly ground black pepper.
3 Heat 25 g /1 oz butter and 30 ml /2 tbls olive oil in a frying-pan. Add the lamb rolls, turning them until well browned on all sides, about 4–6 minutes. Remove from the heat and cut the rolls to make 8 medallions, each approximately 25 mm /1 in thick.
4 When ready to serve, heat another 25 g /1 oz butter and the remaining olive oil in the pan and sauté the medallions for 3 minutes on each side. Remove from the pan with a slotted spoon, arrange the lamb medallions down the centre of a heated serving dish and keep them warm.
5 In a heavy-based pan, melt the remaining butter, add the lemon juice and chopped mint. Finally, stir in the quick meat glaze. Pour the sauce over the lamb medallions and garnish with mint leaves. Serve immediately.

25 minutes making glaze, then 30 minutes   Château Palmer

Courgette purée in potato baskets

Serves 4
900 g /2 lb courgettes
salt and ground black pepper
75 g /3 oz butter
To garnish
4 tomato roses
4 sprigs of parsley

For the potato baskets
450 g /1 lb even-sized floury
* potatoes*
oil, for deep frying
salt
freshly ground black pepper

1 Peel the courgettes and cut them into small dice. Place in a colander and sprinkle with salt. Leave to stand for 30 minutes so that the bitter juices drain away.
2 Meanwhile, begin preparing the potato baskets. Peel the potatoes and cut them into paper-thin slices, using a food processor or mandolin cutter. Cut the slices into julienne strips.
3 Rinse the courgettes under cold running water. Drain well.
4 In a heavy-based saucepan, heat half the butter, then add the prepared courgettes. Season with a little salt and freshly ground black pepper to taste. Cook over a low heat for 20 minutes, or until the courgettes are tender and the liquid has evaporated, stirring occasionally with a wooden spoon.
5 Meanwhile, in a deep-fat frier, heat the oil to 200C /400F or until a cube of day-old bread browns in 40 seconds. Line a small wire mesh ladle, about 6.5 cm /2½ in in diameter, with a thin layer of potato strips. Place another ladle of the same size on top so that the potato strips are held between the two.
6 Deep fry one potato basket for 1–2 minutes, or until crisp and golden. Remove from the ladle and drain well on absorbent paper. Keep warm while you prepare and fry 3 more baskets. Season to taste with salt and black pepper. Keep warm.
7 Press the courgettes through a sieve into a bowl. Stir in the remaining butter. Adjust the seasoning.
8 Divide the mixture among the potato baskets, spooning it in evenly. Arrange on a heated serving plate and serve immediately, garnished with tomato roses and sprigs of parsley.

● Small wire mesh ladles can be bought from Chinese supermarkets or from kitchen equipment stores. The Chinese ones are often sold in packets of 6 or 12, so you can prepare 3 or 4 potato baskets at a time. Once fried, the potato baskets will stay crisp and warm in the oven.

30 minutes draining, then 30 minutes

Gratin dauphinois

Serves 4
700 g /1½ lb new potatoes
about 100 g /4 oz butter
150 ml /5 fl oz thick cream
50 g /2 oz Gruyère cheese, grated
30 ml /2 tbls grated Parmesan cheese
salt and freshly ground black pepper

1 Generously butter a shallow flameproof casserole or deep gratin dish.
2 Peel and slice the potatoes thinly and soak in cold water for a few minutes. Drain and dry thoroughly with a clean tea-towel. Heat the oven to 170C /325F /gas 3.
3 Place a layer of sliced potatoes in overlapping rows on the bottom of the dish. Pour over a quarter of the cream, sprinkle with 30 ml /2 tbls grated cheese (mixed Gruyère and Parmesan), dot with butter and season to taste with salt and freshly ground black pepper. Continue this process until the dish is full, finishing with a layer of grated cheese.
4 Dot with butter and cook in the oven for about 1–1¼ hours, or until the potatoes are cooked through. If the top becomes too brown, cover it with foil. Serve very hot.

Braised chicory with orange

Serves 4
4 large heads of chicory
25 g /1 oz butter
salt and freshly ground black pepper
grated zest and juice of 1½ oranges

1 Heat the oven to 170C /325F /gas 3.
2 Wipe the chicory with a damp cloth and remove any damaged outer leaves. With the point of a sharp knife, scoop out the dense white core at the bottom of each head of chicory.
3 Butter a shallow casserole or a gratin dish large enough to take the chicory comfortably in one layer.
4 Lay the chicory heads side by side in the dish and season to taste with salt and freshly ground black pepper. Sprinkle with the grated orange zest and pour the orange juice over the top.
5 Cover with a lid or foil and cook in the oven for 1¾–2 hours, or until really tender. Serve as soon as possible.

● Cooked chicory tends to turn an unattractive shade of grey if left to stand so it should be served very promptly.

1½ hours

2 hours 10 minutes

Strawberry water-ice with Grand Marnier

Serves 4
350 g /12 oz strawberries
175 g /6 oz sugar
60 ml /4 tbls Grand Marnier
4 strawberries, halved, to decorate
Cigarettes russes, to serve (see recipe)

1 If using the freezer compartment of the refrigerator, turn it down to its lowest temperature, that is, the highest setting, about 1 hour before you start.
2 In a blender, purée the strawberries in 2 batches until smooth. Using the back of a wooden spoon, press the purée through a fine sieve into a bowl, to get rid of the pips.
3 Put the sugar and 425 ml /15 fl oz of water in a heavy-based saucepan and heat gently, stirring, until the sugar is dissolved, then boil for 10 minutes. Leave to become cold.
4 Combine the cold sugar syrup with the strawberry purée and stir in the Grand Marnier. Pour it into a shallow freezer-proof container, cover and freeze for 1 hour, or until it is frozen to a depth of about 25 mm /1 in around the sides of the container.
5 Take the ice out of the refrigerator and stir up the mixture vigorously with a fork, then freeze again for 30 minutes. Repeat 2–3 times, until the ice is half frozen.
6 Cover the ice and leave for a further 2–3 hours until it has frozen hard.
7 About 1 hour before serving, transfer it to the main part of the refrigerator to soften slightly.
8 Arrange 2 scoops of water-ice in each of 4 individual glass dishes and decorate with two strawberry halves. Serve immediately with the Cigarettes russes.

 30 minutes, cooling,
then 5–6 hours freezing, and 1 hour softening

Cigarettes russes

Makes 24
butter, for greasing
75 g /3 oz flour
a pinch of salt
175 g /6 oz caster sugar
105 ml /7 tbls melted butter
2.5 ml /½ tsp vanilla essence
4 egg whites

1 Heat the oven to 180C /350F /gas 4. Grease 2–3 baking sheets with butter.
2 Sift the flour with a pinch of salt and the caster sugar into a bowl. Stir in the melted butter and vanilla essence.
3 In a clean dry bowl, whisk the egg whites until stiff but not dry. With a large metal spoon, fold them well into the flour and butter mixture.
4 Make 2–3 biscuits on each prepared baking sheet. Place a tablespoonful of the mixture 7.5 cm /3 in from the next one and use the back of a spoon to spread each one into a 7.5 cm /3 in circle. Bake, one sheet at a time, in the oven for 10 minutes, or until the biscuits are lightly golden in the centre and slightly darker around the edges.
5 Remove the first tray from the oven. Slide a palette knife under the first biscuit, arrange the biscuit, best side upwards, on top of a pencil or the handle of a wooden spoon. With your hand on top, push the sides underneath to overlap and hold for a few seconds until slightly hardened. Then slip the roll off the pencil or handle and put it on a wire rack to cool completely. Repeat with the remaining biscuits.
6 Continue to bake and shape the rest of the biscuit mixture in the same way. Make sure the baking sheets are completely cold before re-using them; if necessary, run cold water down the back of the sheet to cool before spooning more biscuit mixture onto it.

● Do not be tempted to make more than a few biscuits at a time, even though this means waiting longer while they all bake. Rolling Cigarettes russes can be tricky; if they harden too much before you start rolling them, slip them back in the oven for a minute or two to soften them again.

2 hours

Beef

TRY A GOURMET TREAT!

Celeriac is a much neglected vegetable outside Eastern Europe and France, where it is deservedly popular. Sometimes known as turnip-rooted celery, its texture and flavour are reminiscent of the more familiar stick celery, but with more depth. Unlike stick celery, it is tough and can be indigestible raw, so it is best blanched first when served as a salad. Try it in my recipe with a tangy mustard mayonnaise, adding the dressing while the celeriac is still slightly warm so that it absorbs the mustardy flavour. While I would advise you to make your own mayonnaise for best results, you can substitute a good quality commercial brand instead.

Boeuf à la ficelle is impossible to translate literally; *ficelle* means string, and the dish takes its name from the string tied around the beef as it poaches gently in a well-flavoured stock. It is a dish for those who like the traditional flavour of boiled beef — but gourmet-style, using the most tender of tournedos steaks. Like pan-fried or grilled steaks, I think tournedos *à la ficelle* are best cooked rare, but you can adjust the cooking time to suit your own and your guests' tastes. Serve the steaks with vegetables cooked in the same stock, and spark the flavour just before serving with lots of freshly ground black pepper and a good sprinkling of brandy over each individual steak.

The beauty of Boeuf à la ficelle is that it comes complete with its own vegetables. Nevertheless, it does need other accompaniments, and what better than delicious Sautéed courgettes complemented by crisp Pommes au beurre. As a decorative touch to the courgettes, use a potato peeler to peel off thin strips of skin lengthways so that the courgettes are striped alternately green and white.

I have an especially soft spot for rich, chocolaty desserts and Chocolate fancy cake is just the thing to reach that spot! You will find, too, that guests who usually never touch a dessert just cannot refuse the delights of this one. A light cake flavoured with melted plain chocolate, it is layered with lashings of sweetened whipped cream and decorated with the most beautiful chocolate caraque. These elegant curls are made from chocolate which has been melted in a bowl set over a pan of hot but not boiling water. A thin layer of the chocolate is then spread onto an oiled surface and left until it is cold when it is shaved into long curls with a small, sharp knife. If you are very pushed for time, you can always use grated chocolate instead of caraque, or else crumble up flaked chocolate.

Celeriac salad with mustard mayonnaise

Bœuf à la ficelle

Sautéed courgettes

Pommes au beurre

Chocolate fancy cake

Wine: Paul Masson red

Plan-ahead timetable

On the day before the meal
Bœuf à la ficelle: make the beef stock, if using home-made.

On the morning of the meal
Chocolate fancy cake: bake and leave it to get cold. Make the chocolate caraque.

Two hours before the meal
Celeriac salad with mustard mayonnaise: prepare the celeriac. Make the mayonnaise.
Bœuf à la ficelle: prepare and cook the vegetables. Reserve. Prepare the tournedos steaks.
Pommes au beurre: prepare the potatoes and soak in iced water.

One hour before the meal
Chocolate fancy cake: make the filling. Assemble, glaze and decorate the cake.
Pommes au beurre: deep fry the potato balls in batches, then set them aside to drain on absorbent paper.

Thirty minutes before the meal
Celeriac salad with mustard mayonnaise: blanch the celeriac. Leave to cool until it is lukewarm. Fold the mustard mayonnaise into the celeriac, then transfer it to a serving dish.
Sautéed courgettes: blanch, then sauté until tender. Keep warm.

Just before the meal
Celeriac salad with mustard mayonnaise: garnish and serve.

Between the first and the main course
Bœuf à la ficelle: cook the steaks and reheat the vegetables. Assemble, season and serve.
Pommes au beurre: sauté the potatoes until browned and cooked through, sprinkle with parsley and serve.
Sautéed courgettes: season, sprinkle with parsley and toss in hot butter before serving.

Celeriac salad with mustard mayonnaise

Serves 4
350–400 g /12–14 oz celeriac
salt
10 ml /2 tsp Dijon mustard
freshly ground black pepper
celery leaves, to garnish
For the mayonnaise (makes about 275 ml /10 fl oz)
2 medium-sized egg yolks
2.5 ml /½ tsp Dijon mustard
salt and freshly ground black pepper
10–15 ml /2–3 tsp lemon juice
275 ml /10 fl oz olive oil

1 Peel and wash the celeriac. Cut it into 4 cm /1½ in lengths, then cut the lengths into 3 mm /⅛ in thick matchstick strips.
2 Put the celeriac strips in a saucepan and cover them with cold water. Season with a good pinch of salt and bring to the boil over a moderate heat. Simmer the celeriac for 3 minutes, or until it is cooked but still firm. Drain well and leave to cool.
3 Meanwhile, make the mayonnaise: place the egg yolks in a small mixing bowl or pudding bowl with the mustard and salt and pepper to taste. Wring out a cloth in very cold water and twist it around the bottom of the bowl to keep it steady and cool.
4 Use a rotary whisk (or a wire whisk or fork) to beat the yolk mixture to a smooth paste. Add a little lemon juice.
5 Add about 50 ml /2 fl oz of the olive oil, drop by drop, beating continuously. Add a little more lemon juice, then some more oil, beating all the time.
6 Continue adding the oil in a thin stream, beating continuously, until the mayonnaise is really thick. Season to taste with salt, pepper and lemon juice, if necessary.
7 When the celeriac has cooled but is still lukewarm, stir the 10 ml /2 tsp mustard into the mayonnaise. Adjust the seasoning, adding more salt and black pepper, if necessary.
8 Using a large metal spoon, fold the mayonnaise into the celeriac matchsticks.
9 Transfer the salad to a serving dish. Garnish it with celery leaves and serve as soon as possible.

 30 minutes, plus cooling

Boeuf à la ficelle

Serves 4

4×175 g /6 oz tournedos
  steaks, 4 cm /1½ in thick
450 g /1 lb carrots
450 g /1 lb small turnips
1.1 L /2 pt well-flavoured
  beef stock, home-made or
  from a cube

225 g /8 oz white button
  mushrooms
4 thin strips of pork fat
freshly ground black pepper
20 ml /4 tsp brandy
finely chopped fresh parsley
bouquet of parsley, to garnish

1 Peel the carrots, then cut them into 4 cm /1½ in segments. Slice each segment lengthways into 5 mm /¼ in thick slices, then cut each slice into 5 mm /¼ in wide strips. Peel the turnips and cut them into strips of the same size.
2 Select a wide saucepan which will take the steaks comfortably side by side. Pour in the stock and add the carrot strips. Bring to the boil, then reduce the heat and simmer for 4 minutes. Add the turnip strips and simmer for 4 minutes longer.
3 Meanwhile, wipe the mushrooms and trim the stems.
4 Add the prepared mushrooms to the pan and simmer gently for 4–5 minutes, or until the vegetables are tender.
5 Using a slotted spoon, transfer the vegetables to a bowl. Pour over a little of the stock and reserve. Keep the remaining stock simmering, if intending to cook the steaks immediately.
6 Wrap a thin strip of pork fat around the middle of each tournedos. Cut 4 pieces of string, each long enough to go round a tournedos and hang over the side of the pan when the tournedos is submerged in stock. Tie one end of each string firmly around each tournedos to keep the strip of pork fat in place.
7 Just before serving, bring the stock to the boil and lower in the tournedos steaks side by side, letting the strings hang over the edge of the pan. Simmer for 5 minutes for rare, 8 minutes for medium and 12 minutes for well done.
8 When the tournedos are ready, pull them out by their strings. Drop the reserved vegetables into the simmering stock to reheat.
9 Remove the strings and strips of pork fat from the tournedos and arrange the steaks on a heated, shallow serving dish.
10 Season each steak generously with freshly ground black pepper and sprinkle each with a teaspoon of brandy. Using a slotted spoon, transfer the vegetables to the dish, arranging them around the steaks. Moisten the vegetables with some of the cooking stock and sprinkle with finely chopped parsley. Serve immediately, garnished with the parsley. Reserve the remaining stock for another recipe.

preparing the vegetables,
then 25 minutes

carafe of Paul Masson
red wine

Sautéed courgettes

Serves 4

1 kg /2 lb small courgettes
salt
75–100 g /3–4 oz butter
coarse salt and freshly ground black pepper
finely chopped fresh parsley

1 Wipe the courgettes clean and trim the ends. Using a potato peeler, peel off thin strips lengthways so that you have alternating bands of white and green along the length of each courgette.
2 Drop the courgettes into a pan of cold salted water. Bring to the boil, cover and simmer for just 5 minutes, then drain thoroughly.
3 In a large sauté pan, or deep, heavy-bottomed frying-pan with a lid, heat the butter until it just begins to bubble. Lay the courgettes in it, side by side, in one layer. Cover the pan and simmer over a medium heat for 10–15 minutes, shaking the pan occasionally, until the courgettes are tender (but not disintegrating). They should be a light golden colour all over.
4 Season with coarse salt and freshly ground black pepper. Sprinkle the courgettes with some finely chopped parsley and toss them once more in the butter before serving.

30 minutes

Pommes au beurre

Serves 4
1 kg /2 lb potatoes
oil, for deep frying
salt and freshly ground black pepper
25 g /1 oz butter
30 ml /2 tbls olive oil
finely chopped fresh parsley

1 Peel the potatoes and cut them into small balls with a melon-baller or vegetable cutter. Soak the balls in iced water for 1 hour.
2 Dry the potato balls well on absorbent paper.
3 Heat the oil in a large frying-pan or deep-fat frier to 190C /375F — at this temperature a cube of bread will brown in 50 seconds. Fry the potato balls in batches until golden, about 5 minutes per batch. Remove them with a slotted spoon and drain them on absorbent paper. Season the potato balls generously with salt and freshly ground black pepper.
4 Just before serving, sauté the potato balls in the butter and olive oil for about 5 minutes until brown and cooked through.
5 Drain them on absorbent paper, then sprinkle them with finely chopped fresh parsley and serve as soon as possible.

● Frying twice is the secret of really successful French-fried potatoes. It is also an easy way to produce perfect fried potatoes when you have guests to entertain. The French describe these delicious potato balls simply as 'cooked in butter'. Left-over bits and pieces of potato can be used for a purée or for thickening soups. Keep the potato balls covered with water until you cook them or they will discolour, but try to use them within a few hours.

⁍ 1 hour soaking,
then 20 minutes

Chocolate fancy cake

Serves 4–8
butter and flour for the cake tin
175 g /6 oz softened butter
160 g /5½ oz caster sugar
175 g /6 oz plain chocolate, melted
  and cooled
6 egg yolks
8 egg whites
75 g /3 oz flour
a pinch of salt
25 g /1 oz cocoa powder

For the cream filling
425 ml /15 fl oz thick cream
15 ml /1 tbls caster sugar
2 drops vanilla essence
For the apricot glaze
45 ml /3 tbls apricot jam
15 ml /1 tbls lemon juice
For the decoration
caraque, made with 225 g /
  8 oz plain chocolae
icing sugar

1 Heat the oven to 150C /300F /gas 2. Choose a cake tin 20 cm /8 in in diameter and 6.5 cm /2½ in deep and cut a circle of greaseproof paper to line the bottom. Lightly butter and flour the paper and tin.
2 In a large bowl, with a wooden spoon, cream the butter, gradually adding 75 g /3 oz sugar. Beat until light and fluffy. Stir in the chocolate, then beat in the egg yolks, one at a time.
3 In a clean, dry bowl, whisk the egg whites to soft peaks. Whisk in the remaining sugar, 15 ml /1 tbls at a time. Continue whisking until the mixture is glossy and stands in soft peaks again.
4 Sift the flour, salt and cocoa powder onto a sheet of greaseproof paper. With a large metal spoon, fold ⅓ of the egg white mixture, then ⅓ of the flour mixture into the chocolate mixture. Repeat until all the ingredients are incorporated, then blend, beating lightly with a wooden spoon. Spoon the mixture into the tin and bake for 1–1¼ hours. A skewer inserted into the centre should come out clean.
5 Leave to cool in the tin for 5 minutes, then run a sharp knife around the inside of the tin and turn out the cake onto a wire rack. Leave it to get cold.
6 Make the filling: in a bowl, whisk the cream, sugar and vanilla essence to soft peaks. Horizontally cut the cake into 3 layers. Place the bottom layer of cake on a serving dish and spread evenly with half the cream. Place the second layer on top and repeat. Cover with the third layer, smoothing away any cream that has oozed out.
7 In a small saucepan, bring the apricot jam and lemon juice to the boil, stirring to blend with a wooden spoon. Brush the glaze over the top and sides of the cake.
8 Reserve the best caraque curls for the cake top. With a palette knife, carefully pat on caraque curls to cover the cake sides thickly. Lay the remaining caraque neatly on top to cover the cake. Dust with icing sugar and serve as soon as possible.

 2½ hours, plus cooling,
and making the caraque

FOOD FOR HEARTY APPETITES

Twin vegetable pâté

~

Flemish carbonnade of beef

Pea, corn and onion hotpot

Granny's grated potatoes

~

Sweet cheese crêpes

Wine: Cos d'Estournel or another St Estèphe

Plan-ahead timetable

On the day before the meal
Twin vegetable pâté: make the purées, combine to make the pâté and chill.

On the morning of the meal
Sweet cheese crêpes: make the batter, rest it for 2 hours, then make the crêpes, fill and chill.

Three hours before the meal
Flemish carbonnade of beef: make and cook the carbonnade. Keep hot.

One and a quarter hours before the meal
Twin vegetable pâté: unmould the pâté and garnish.
Granny's grated potatoes: prepare the potato mixture; make

An informal 'serve yourself' dinner in Flemish country-style is welcome after a brisk day's activity. A hearty appetizer and casserole for the main course make up the body of the meal. Twin vegetable pâté served chilled with slices of hot toast and a plate of butter balls makes an elegant but easily prepared appetizer. Well-flavoured purées of carrot and mushroom are moulded together, combining flavour and colour to make an unusual pâté.

The Flemish carbonnade of beef is the centrepiece of the menu — it is easy to cook in advance and serve from the sideboard, or right from the table. Braising beef, cooked to succulent tenderness in stock and pale ale and then served with the thickened cooking juices, makes a really warming, rustic stew. The carbonnade is delicious served with side dishes of Pea, corn and onion hotpot and Granny's grated potatoes. Pea, corn and onion hotpot is a colourful combination of vegetables served in a creamy sauce to make a substantial accompaniment. Granny's grated potatoes take me straight back to my childhood. I can still smell the tempting aroma of those sizzling potato cakes as they cooked on my granny's range.

End the meal with something typically Flemish for dessert — Sweet cheese crêpes: crêpes filled with a mixture of three soft cheeses and vanilla, and served with a rich brandy-flavoured chocolate sauce.

If you are a beginner at giving dinner parties, this menu is tailor-made for you. You should be able to get your timing just right as nearly all the food can be made well ahead — even the day before — without the quality being affected. The Flemish carbonnade stays at the right temperature in the lowest of ovens while you and your guests enjoy your pre-dinner drinks and the first course. The vegetables, too, will hold their own in a pan without the lid.

I would serve Cos d'Estournel or another wine from St Estèphe, but beer would be acceptable as the main course is cooked with beer.

and cook the potato cake. Then keep it warm in a low oven.
Pea, corn and onion hotpot: prepare the sauce and cook the peas.

Ten minutes before the meal
Sweet cheese crêpes: make the chocolate sauce and keep warm.
Pea, corn and onion hotpot: add the peas, cream and corn to the
sauce and heat through.
Twin vegetable pâté: make the toast.

Just before the main course
Flemish carbonnade of beef: thicken with *beurre manié*.
Granny's grated potatoes: turn out onto a serving platter and pour
hot, melted butter over the top.

Between the main course and the dessert
Sweet cheese crêpes: put into the oven for 10 minutes to warm
through and serve.

Twin vegetable pâté

Serves 6

350 g /12 oz carrots, sliced
salt
150 g /5 oz butter, softened
30 ml /2 tbls finely chopped dill
1 medium-sized onion, finely
  chopped
2 garlic cloves, finely chopped
5 ml /1 tsp curry paste
freshly ground black pepper
60 ml /4 tbls chopped salted
  cashew nuts

225 g /8 oz mushrooms, finely
  chopped
60 ml /4 tbls freshly grated
  Parmesan cheese
butter, for greasing
To garnish
4 carrot leaves (in season)
  or flat-leaved parsley
8 carrot 'flowers'
To serve
hot toast and chilled butter

1 Bring a saucepan of salted water to the boil and add the sliced
carrots. Cook for 15 minutes, or until tender. In a small bowl, work
75 g /3 oz softened butter with the finely chopped dill until well
blended. Set aside.
2 Melt 25 g /1 oz butter in a saucepan. Add half the finely chopped
onion, 1 garlic clove and 2.5 ml /½ tsp curry paste. Cook over a
moderate heat for 10 minutes, stirring occasionally, until the onion is
soft. Remove from the heat. Add the drained carrots and half the dill
butter and season to taste with salt and black pepper.
3 Purée the mixture in a blender or a food processor until smooth, or
press it through a food mill. Transfer the purée to a bowl and stir in
the chopped nuts.
4 In another saucepan, melt the remaining butter. Add the remaining
onion, garlic and curry paste. Cook over moderate heat for 10 minutes,
stirring occasionally, until the onion is soft. Add the chopped
mushrooms and cook over a high heat for 5 minutes, stirring
constantly, until the mushrooms are soft and the moisture reduced.
5 Remove the pan from the heat, add the remaining dill butter and
season with salt and freshly ground black pepper to taste. Purée the
mixture in a food processor until smooth, or press it through a food
mill. Transfer the puréed mixture to a bowl and stir in the grated
Parmesan cheese.
6 Butter an 850 ml /1½ pt loaf tin or mould and spoon in the carrot
mixture. Level the top with a palette knife. Spoon the mushroom
mixture on top and level again with the knife. Chill for 3 hours, or
until firmly set.
7 Unmould the pâté onto a flat serving platter. Garnish with carrot
leaves or flat-leaved parsley and arrange the carrot flowers around the
pâté. Serve with hot toast and chilled butter.

 1 hour,
plus 3 hours chilling

Flemish carbonnade of beef

Serves 6
1 kg /2 lb braising beef
salt and freshly ground black pepper
40 g /1½ oz butter
45 ml /3 tbls olive oil
2 Spanish onions, thinly sliced
15 ml /1 tbls wine vinegar
15 ml /1 tbls light brown sugar
200 ml /7 fl oz beef stock, home-made or from a cube
275 ml /10 fl oz pale ale
1 bouquet garni
40 g /1½ oz beurre manié (made by mashing 20 g /¾ oz butter with
    20 ml /1½ tbls flour)
flat-leaved parsley, to garnish
lemon slice, to garnish

1   Cut the beef across the grain into fairly thin slices. Season
generously with salt and freshly ground black pepper.
2   Heat the butter and olive oil in a large flameproof casserole. When
the foaming subsides, put in a few slices of beef and brown them.
Remove from the casserole with a slotted spoon and keep warm. Repeat
with the remaining meat.
3   Add the sliced onions to the fat remaining in the casserole. Sauté
over a moderate heat, stirring occasionally, for 10 minutes, or until the
onions are a rich golden brown. Return the beef slices, add the wine
vinegar and brown sugar and cook for a further 1–2 minutes, stirring.
4   Add the beef stock, pale ale and bouquet garni and season with salt
and freshly ground black pepper to taste. Cover and simmer gently for
2 hours, or until the beef is tender, stirring occasionally.
5   Add the beurre manié to the carbonnade, a little at a time,
stirring constantly. Simmer gently for 1–2 minutes, or until the
liquid has thickened. Adjust the seasoning, garnish and serve
immediately.

 30 minutes,
then 2 hours cooking

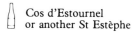 Cos d'Estournel
or another St Estèphe

Pea, corn and onion hotpot

Serves 6
25 g /1 oz butter
30 ml /2 tbls olive oil
1 large Spanish onion, finely chopped
22.5 ml /1½ tbls flour
150 ml /5 fl oz chicken stock, home-made or from a cube
salt and freshly ground black pepper
1.5 ml /¼ tsp cayenne pepper
275 g /10 oz frozen peas
350 g /12 oz canned sweetcorn kernels, drained
150 ml /5 fl oz thick cream
a pinch of cayenne pepper
parsley sprig, to garnish

1   Heat the butter and olive oil in a saucepan. Add the finely chopped
onion and cook over moderate heat for 10 minutes, or until soft but not
coloured, stirring occasionally.
2   Stir in the flour and cook for a further 2–3 minutes, or until lightly
coloured, stirring frequently.
3   Gradually pour in the chicken stock, stirring vigorously with
a whisk to prevent lumps from forming. Bring to the boil and simmer
for 2–3 minutes. Season with salt and freshly ground black pepper to
taste, and add the cayenne pepper. Remove the hotpot from the heat
and keep warm.
4   Bring a saucepan of salted water to the boil, add the peas and bring
back to the boil. Reduce the heat and simmer gently for 2–3 minutes.
Drain and keep warm.
5   Add the peas, cream and corn to the sauce and stir over low heat
until the mixture is heated through. Adjust the seasoning, pour into a
heated serving dish, sprinkle with a pinch of cayenne pepper and
garnish with a sprig of parsley, then serve immediately.

 30 minutes

Granny's grated potatoes

Serves 6
900 g /2 lb potatoes, grated
4 fresh eggs, beaten
60 ml /4 tbls finely chopped fresh parsley
2 garlic cloves, finely chopped
salt and freshly ground black pepper
50 g /2 oz butter
30 ml /2 tbls olive oil
50 g /2 oz butter, melted (optional)

1 In a large bowl, mix together the grated potatoes, eggs, parsley and garlic. Season with salt and freshly ground black pepper to taste.
2 Heat 40 g /1½ oz of the butter and 15 ml /1 tbls of the olive oil in a large frying-pan. When the foaming subsides, spread the potato mixture evenly in the pan, using a palette knife. Cook over high heat for 2–3 minutes to brown the underside. Reduce the heat and cook for a further 5–7 minutes, or until the potato mixture is firm on one side.
3 Turn the cake over using two spatulas or palette knives. Increase the heat to high, ease a palette knife under the potato cake and add the remaining butter and olive oil. Cook for 2–3 minutes to brown the second side. Reduce the heat and cook for a further 5–7 minutes, or until the potato cake is tender and set. Turn it out onto a large, heated serving platter and serve.

● If you do not serve this dish immediately, you can keep it warm, then pour hot melted butter over it just before serving.

30–35 minutes

Sweet cheese crêpes

Serves 6
75 g /3 oz flour
2.5 ml /½ tsp salt
2 medium-sized eggs, beaten
30 ml /2 tbls melted butter or oil
150 ml /5 fl oz milk
oil, for frying
For the filling
90 ml /6 tbls caster sugar
3 egg yolks
350 g /12 oz cottage cheese, drained and sieved
175 g /6 oz Ricotta cheese, sieved
175 g /6 oz cream cheese, sieved
4 ml /¾ tsp vanilla essence
For the chocolate sauce
175 g /6 oz plain chocolate
225 ml /8 fl oz thick cream
30 ml /2 tbls brandy

1 Prepare the crêpe batter. Sift the flour and salt into a bowl and stir in the beaten eggs and melted butter or oil. Gradually add the milk. Strain if lumpy and leave to stand for 2 hours.
2 Heat a 12 cm /5 in diameter pan and grease it with a wad of absorbent paper soaked in oil. Add 30 ml /2 tbls batter and tilt the pan to cover the surface. Cook for 1 minute on each side. As the crêpes are cooked, stack them, then cover with foil. Make 12 crêpes.
3 In a bowl, combine the caster sugar, egg yolks, cottage cheese, Ricotta cheese, cream cheese and vanilla essence. Beat until smooth. Chill for 30 minutes in the refrigerator to harden the mixture.
4 Meanwhile, make the chocolate sauce. Put the chocolate, thick cream and brandy in the top of a double boiler. Place over hot but not boiling water and beat constantly with a whisk until the chocolate has melted and the sauce is well blended. Remove from the heat but leave the sauce over the hot water to keep warm.
5 Heat the oven to 180C /350F /gas 4. Divide the chilled cheese mixture evenly among the crêpes. Roll them up and transfer to a shallow ovenproof dish large enough to take the crêpe rolls in one layer. Bake for 10 minutes, or until warmed through.
6 Transfer the crêpes to individual plates. Pour a little of the warm chocolate sauce over the crêpes and the rest into a warmed jug. Serve immediately.

making the batter and standing, then 1 hour, plus chilling

STEAKS WITH A DIFFERENCE

Cream of cauliflower soup

Pan-fried sirloin
with mustard glaze

Sautéed potatoes with onion

Brussels sprouts
à la polonaise

Adam and Eve pudding

Wine: Côtes-du-Rhône-Villages

Plan-ahead timetable

Two and a half hours before the meal
Cream of cauliflower soup: make the soup, sieve and cool.
Pan-fried sirloin with mustard glaze: prepare the garnish.

One and a half hours before the meal
Brussels sprouts à la polonaise: wash and trim the Brussels sprouts. Hard boil the egg.
Adam and Eve pudding: prepare the fruit, bake with the walnuts and reserve.

One hour before the meal
Pan-fried sirloin with mustard glaze: bring the steaks to room temperature.
Adam and Eve pudding: prepare topping. Whip and chill cream.
Sautéed potatoes with onion: peel and slice the potatoes; keep them in water until needed.

Thirty minutes before the meal
Adam and Eve pudding: add the topping and bake.
Brussels sprouts à la polonaise: cook the sprouts until just tender, drain them, season with salt and pepper and keep warm.

If you like steak, I think you will appreciate this version that I first tasted in a small English pub in the Thames Valley. Prime-quality sirloin steaks are pan-fried in a little butter and oil and then finished off in a most unusual way — spread with Dijon mustard, sprinkled with brown sugar and glazed under the grill. The result is a delicious, bubbling golden steak. The garnish for this dish is special, too. Delicately trimmed minaret mushrooms and sculptured tomato waterlilies teamed with sprigs of watercress make an appealing trio.

I like to serve these steaks with two vegetables — thinly sliced potatoes sautéed in butter with finely chopped onions, and a generous helping of Brussels sprouts à la polonaise. Use tiny Brussels sprouts — if the sprouts are larger than you wish, just peel off the outer layers until they are the size you want. Simmer them until tender but crisp in boiling salted water and then dress them with grated lemon zest, finely chopped parsley and chopped egg white and glaze with lightly browned butter. A squeeze of lemon juice is added at the last moment to marry the flavours.

Precede the main course with a subtly flavoured Cream of cauliflower soup. This is one of those wonderful home-made soups that takes an ordinary vegetable and turns it into something quite irresistible. The cauliflower is enhanced with onion, celery and parsley, then blended until smooth and enriched with an egg yolk and cream liaison.

I think a comforting family pudding makes the perfect ending to this meal, and what better choice than Adam and Eve pudding. This has long been one of my favourite 'puds'. In this recipe I have used fresh apples flavoured with orange and lemon juice, clove and cinnamon and sprinkled with walnuts. Fresh pears are equally delicious but you can use canned or bottled fruit. Whatever you use as the filling, the topping for this traditional pudding will always be the same — light, spongy, golden and delicious.

Sautéed potatoes with onion: cook the onions and garlic in butter until soft, then reserve.

Fifteen minutes before the meal
Cream of cauliflower soup: reheat the soup, add the liaison and season. Prepare the garnish.
Sautéed potatoes with onion: drain and dry the potatoes; sauté them in butter until golden, then add the onions and garlic.
Pan-fried sirloin with mustard glaze: season the steaks.

Just before the meal
Cream of cauliflower soup: add the garnishes and serve.
Adam and Eve pudding: turn off the oven but leave the pudding in it to keep warm.

Between the first and the main course
Pan-fried sirloin with mustard glaze: cook and glaze the steak. Garnish the steak with the tomatoes and mushrooms.
Brussels sprouts à la polonaise: heat butter; garnish and serve.
Sautéed potatoes with onion: garnish and serve.

Between the main course and the dessert
Adam and Eve pudding: sprinkle with icing sugar and serve with chilled whipped cream.

Cream of cauliflower soup

Serves 4

1 cauliflower, weighing about
   1 kg /2 lb
salt
50 g /2 oz butter
60 ml /4 tbls flour
850 ml /1½ pt hot chicken
   stock, home-made or from
   a cube
1 onion, coarsely chopped
1 celery stick, coarsely chopped

15 ml /1 tbls freshly chopped
   parsley
2 medium-sized egg yolks
150 ml /5 fl oz thick cream
freshly ground black pepper
freshly grated nutmeg
For the garnish
4 thin lemon slices
thick cream, whisked with a
   pinch of salt
finely chopped fresh parsley

1 Trim the outer leaves and stalks from the cauliflower and break into florets. Poach the florets in boiling salted water for 5 minutes; drain and reserve.
2 Melt the butter in a heavy-based saucepan; away from the heat, stir in the flour. Return to a low heat and stir for 1–2 minutes until smooth. Remove from the heat and gradually stir in the hot chicken stock. Add the chopped onion, celery and parsley. Return to a low heat and simmer for 20 minutes.
3 Strain the flavoured sauce and return it to the cleaned pan; add the cauliflower florets and simmer until tender. Blend the mixture or press it through a fine sieve. Return the soup to the pan and reheat gently.
4 Lightly beat together the egg yolks and thick cream; stir in 45 ml /3 tbls of the hot soup, then pour the mixture into the pan. Cook gently, stirring, for about 3 minutes, or until thickened, taking care not to allow the soup to come to the boil. Season to taste with salt, freshly ground black pepper and a little grated nutmeg.
5 Ladle the soup into a warmed serving bowl. Garnish with lemon slices topped with salted whipped cream and a sprinkling of finely chopped parsley.

1 hour

Pan-fried sirloin with mustard glaze

Serves 4
4 × 275 g /10 oz sirloin steaks, trimmed
salt and freshly ground black pepper
75 g /3 oz butter
30 ml /2 tbls olive oil
15 ml /1 tbls Dijon mustard
30 ml /2 tbls brown sugar
For the garnish
8 minaret mushrooms, see note below
4 tomato waterlilies, see note below
sprigs of watercress

1 Season the steaks generously with freshly ground black pepper and
let them come to room temperature.
2 Heat the grill to high. Heat 50 g /2 oz of the butter and the olive oil
in a thick-bottomed frying-pan. Season the steaks with salt and more
freshly ground black pepper and sauté on each side. The frying time
depends on how you want the steaks: for blue, cook them for 1¼
minutes each side; for rare, 3 minutes each side; for medium, 4–5
minutes each side; and for well done, 6–7 minutes each side.
3 Meanwhile, in a small pan melt the remaining butter and sauté the
minaret mushrooms. Remove and keep them warm.
4 Spread the mustard on top of the steaks and sprinkle them with
brown sugar. Transfer the steaks and the tomato waterlilies to a
flameproof gratin dish. Cook them under the grill for 3 minutes, or
until the steaks are glazed and golden brown and the tomatoes are
warmed through. Pour off the fat from the pan juices and heat the
remaining juices. Pour these over the steaks and serve immediately,
garnished with the minaret mushrooms, tomato waterlilies and sprigs
of watercress.

● To make the minaret mushrooms, hold the mushroom stalk
downwards and, angling the knife, make a series of shallow cuts from
the top of the cap. The cuts should not meet at the top and they should
be slightly curved. Holding the knife at the opposite angle, make a
second series of cuts close to the first. Remove the strips in between the
cuts. To make tomato waterlilies, cut around the middle of each tomato
in a zig-zag pattern with a small, sharp knife.

bringing the steaks to room
temperature, then 6–20 minutes   Côtes-du-Rhône-Villages

Sautéed potatoes with onion

Serves 4
450–700 g /1–1½ lb even-sized potatoes
50 g /2 oz butter
1 small onion, finely chopped
1 garlic clove, crushed
salt and freshly ground black pepper
30 ml /2 tbls finely chopped fresh parsley

1 Slice the potatoes thinly and soak them in cold water until needed.
Drain them in a colander, then dry the slices thoroughly in a clean tea-
towel or on absorbent paper.
2 Melt 15 g /½ oz butter in a small, heavy-bottomed frying-pan and
fry the finely chopped onion and crushed garlic, stirring occasionally,
over a moderate heat until the onion is cooked and soft but not
coloured.
3 Melt the remaining butter in a large, heavy-bottomed frying-pan.
When hot, add the potatoes and sauté them over a moderate heat,
turning them frequently with a fish slice for 10–15 minutes until they
are lightly golden.
4 Add the softened onion and garlic and cook until the potatoes are
crisp and golden. Season with salt and freshly ground black pepper
to taste.
5 Transfer the potatoes to a heated serving dish. Sprinkle with finely
chopped parsley and serve immediately.

40 minutes

Brussels sprouts à la polonaise

Serves 4
500 g /1 lb Brussels sprouts
salt and freshly ground black pepper
2–3 lemons, thinly sliced
50 g /2 oz butter
coarsely grated zest and juice of 1 lemon
15–30 ml /1–2 tbls finely chopped fresh parsley
white of 1 hard-boiled egg, finely chopped

1 Cut off the stem ends and remove any wilted or damaged outer leaves from the Brussels sprouts. (If the Brussels sprouts are not young, remove the tough outer leaves entirely.) Score a small cross in each stem so that the heat penetrates more easily at the thickest part, allowing them to cook evenly.
2 Drop the sprouts into a large pan of boiling salted water and simmer, uncovered, for 5 minutes. Cover the pan and continue to cook for 5 (if very young) to 15 minutes longer, or until just tender. Drain well and season generously with salt and freshly ground black pepper.
3 Place the lemon slices around the edge of a heated serving dish and arrange the seasoned Brussels sprouts in the centre.
4 Heat the butter in a frying-pan and cook over a medium-high heat until it is lightly browned. Pour it over the sprouts. Sprinkle them with the grated lemon zest, finely chopped parsley and chopped egg white. Add the lemon juice to taste and serve immediately.

● This classic garnish can also be used for cooked asparagus or cauliflower. The sieved egg yolk may also be included for colour contrast.

25–40 minutes

Adam and Eve pudding

Serves 4
1 kg /2 lb dessert apples or ripe pears
juice of 1 small lemon
juice and finely grated zest of ½ orange
1 clove
a pinch of cinnamon
60 ml /4 tbls chopped walnuts
30 ml /2 tbls caster sugar
icing sugar, sifted
chilled whipped cream, to serve
For the topping
100 g /4 oz butter
100 g /4 oz caster sugar
2 eggs, well beaten
100 g /4 oz flour
5 ml /1 tsp baking powder
salt
15–30 ml /1–2 tbls milk

1 Heat the oven to 190C /375F /gas 5. Peel, core and slice the apples or pears thickly into a deep 20 × 25 cm /8 × 10 in baking dish. Add the lemon and orange juice, grated orange zest, clove, a pinch of cinnamon and 30 ml /2 tbls water. Toss well.
2 Sprinkle the apples or pears with the chopped walnuts and caster sugar. Cover the baking dish tightly with foil and bake the fruit in the oven for about 15 minutes while you prepare the topping.
3 To make the topping, cream the butter and caster sugar together in a bowl until light and fluffy. Gradually add the beaten eggs, beating well between each addition.
4 In another bowl, sift the flour with the baking powder and a pinch of salt. Fold this into the creamed mixture alternately with the milk. Mix lightly until the batter is smoothly blended.
5 Spread the batter evenly over the apples or pears and return the dish to the oven for a further 30 minutes, or until the topping is well risen and springy to the touch, with a rich golden top.
6 Just before serving, sprinkle with the icing sugar. This pudding is at its best served warm with chilled whipped cream.

1 hour 10 minutes

Plan-ahead timetable

On the day before the meal
Mexican beans: soak the beans.
Mexican custard tarts: bake the tart cases, cool and keep them in an airtight container.

Four and a half hours before the meal
Mexican scallop seviche (if serving): prepare and marinate the scallops and corals.
Mexican custard tarts: make and chill the custards. Prepare and chill the fruit and liqueurs.

Two hours before the meal
Chili con carne: prepare and simmer the beef.
Mexican beans: cook the beans, drain and reserve.

One and a half hours before the meal
Mexican scallop seviche (if serving): prepare the tomatoes and pepper and add to the scallops. Toss, season and chill.
Raw mushroom and prawn appetizer (if serving): make dressing and marinate the mushrooms. Prepare the prawns.
Chili con carne: add the chilli seasoning and simmer.
Lettuce, watercress and orange salad: prepare and chill the lettuce and watercress. Prepare the oranges and dressing.

A MEMORABLE MEAL – MEXICAN STYLE

Mexican scallop seviche

Raw mushroom and prawn appetizer

Chili con carne

Mexican beans

Lettuce, watercress and orange salad

Mexican custard tarts

To drink: lager

T reat your friends to a meal in the Mexican style — spiced with chilli, then cooled with refreshing fruit. Seviche is a traditional Mexican appetizer of raw fish marinated in citrus juice. My version, for this meal, is made with scallops. Lime juice is normally used, but lemon juice can be used if lime is not available. You will find that the acidity of the fruit juice 'pickles' the scallops and transforms their texture and flavour as though they were cooked. Garnished with a lightly spiced mixture of pepper, avocado and stuffed olives, this unusual starter sets the mood in grand style. Or, if you prefer, serve your guests a Raw mushroom and prawn appetizer. This is not so strongly Mexican in flavour, but the crisp, fresh flavour will still combine well with this meal.

Chili con carne — the Spanish name means chilli with meat — is a familiar dish to many people. Chillies belong to the same family as the sweet pepper, although they certainly carry a much stronger bite. However, it is not necessary to make the food blindingly hot to create an authentic dish and that is why I choose to use Mexican chilli seasoning, which is a strong but pleasant blend of spices, instead of the powdered or fresh chillies. In my recipe for Chili con carne, bite-sized cubes of beef are slowly cooked with spicy Mexican chilli seasoning and flavoured with garlic and oregano. For a real Latin American effect, serve this dish with Mexican beans — red kidney beans cooked with yet more chilli — and pretty yellow Saffron rice. A light, fresh salad of lettuce and watercress with sliced oranges is the perfect counterpart to calm the palate. Why not serve cool pitchers of lager to quench the thirst of your guests.

For dessert give your guests two empty tart shells each, and let them choose their own fillings from a selection of three smooth, flavoured custard creams, and raspberries and strawberries chilled in different liqueurs. These Mexican custard tarts make an exciting finish to a meal that is truly out of the ordinary.

Forty-five minutes before the meal
Mexican beans: make the sauce, add the beans and simmer.

Twenty-five minutes before the meal
Saffron rice: prepare and cook the rice.
Mexican scallop seviche (if serving): assemble and mix.
Raw mushrooms and prawn appetizer (if serving): combine the mushrooms and prawns and assemble the salad.

Between the first and the main course
Saffron rice: top with Mexican beans and serve.
Lettuce, watercress and orange salad: assemble and serve.

Mexican scallop seviche

Serves 4

4 large fresh scallops
juice of 1 lemon or lime
1 small tomato
½ small green pepper
30 ml /2 tbls olive oil
30 ml /2 tbls chopped parsley

30 ml /2 tbls finely chopped
 fresh marjoram
salt and ground black pepper
a dash of Tabasco
1 small ripe avocado
3 stuffed green olives
12 small lettuce leaves

1 To prepare the scallops, clean away the beard which appears behind the coral in a black translucent line, as well as any other black parts. Wash the scallops in cold running water and dry them well with absorbent paper. Cut off the corals, leaving them whole, and cut the whites horizontally into 3 slices.

2 Place the scallop slices and the corals in a bowl. Pour the lemon or lime juice over them and leave to marinate for 3 hours, turning gently from time to time.

3 Put the tomato into a cup. Pour boiling water over it and let it stand for 10 seconds. Remove from the cup and peel off the skin. Then quarter the tomato and discard the seeds and juice. Cut the flesh into 5 mm /¼ in dice. Remove the seeds and white pith from the green pepper, and cut the flesh into 5 mm /¼ in dice.

4 Add the diced tomato flesh and pepper to the marinated scallop slices and corals, together with the olive oil, finely chopped parsley and marjoram. Mix gently but thoroughly and season with salt and freshly ground black pepper and a dash of Tabasco to taste. Chill.

5 Just before serving, peel the avocado carefully and remove the stone. Cut the flesh into small dice. Add to the scallops and vegetables and toss gently until well coated with liquid, to avoid discoloration.

6 Slice the stuffed olives into rings. Add them to the bowl and mix in lightly.

7 Spoon the mixture onto 4 individual serving plates. Arrange 3 lettuce leaves near the edge on one side of each plate, with 1 scallop slice slightly overlapping each leaf. Place a piece of coral in the centre and serve immediately.

preparing and marinating the scallops,
then 15 minutes, plus chilling

Raw mushroom and prawn appetizer

Serves 4

175 g /6 oz button mushrooms
120 ml /8 tbls olive oil
30 ml /2 tbls wine vinegar
1.5 ml /¼ tsp mustard powder
1.5–2.5 ml /¼–½ tsp chopped fresh rosemary or 30 ml /2 tbls
 chopped fresh parsley
salt and freshly ground black pepper
a pinch of sugar
175 g /6 oz boiled peeled prawns
juice of 1 lemon
a pinch of cayenne pepper
lettuce leaves
finely chopped fresh chives or parsley, to garnish

1 Wipe the mushrooms and trim the stalks.

2 To make the dressing, beat the olive oil, wine vinegar and mustard powder in a bowl with a fork until the mixture emulsifies (or shake the ingredients together in a screw-topped jar). Season with the chopped rosemary or parsley, salt, freshly ground black pepper and sugar to taste.

3 Slice the mushrooms thinly and place in the herb-flavoured vinaigrette dressing. Toss until each slice is thoroughly coated. Cover the bowl and leave to marinate for 1 hour.

4 Meanwhile, place the peeled prawns in a small bowl. Add the lemon juice, salt, freshly ground pepper and cayenne pepper to taste and stir to mix.

5 When ready to serve, line a shallow dish with lettuce leaves. Drain the prawns and add to the mushrooms. Toss well and pile into the middle of the dish, sprinkle with finely chopped chives or parsley and serve immediately.

● If you are buying freshly boiled unpeeled prawns for this dish, you will need to buy 350 g /12 oz. It is a good idea to reserve one or more unpeeled prawns for a garnish.

20 minutes,
plus 1 hour marinating

Chili con carne

Serves 4
900 g /2 lb lean braising steak
60 ml /4 tbls bacon fat or
dripping
1 Spanish onion, finely chopped
4 garlic cloves, finely chopped
425 ml /15 fl oz well-flavoured
beef stock, home-made or
from a cube
150 ml /5 fl oz red wine
45 ml /3 tbls Mexican chilli
seasoning

15 ml /1 tbls flour
2 bay leaves
2.5 ml /½ tsp cumin powder
2.5 ml /½ tsp dried oregano
salt and freshly ground black
pepper
bay leaves, to garnish (optional)
strips of chilli, to garnish
(optional)
To serve
Mexican beans, see recipe
Saffron rice, see recipe

1   Cut the beef into bite-sized cubes, trimming off any excess fat. Heat the bacon fat or dripping in a large, flameproof casserole over a high heat. Add half the meat cubes and sauté for 6–8 minutes, turning occasionally until evenly browned. Remove the browned beef cubes with a slotted spoon and keep warm while you sauté the second batch. Remove the second batch and keep warm with the first batch.
2   Sauté the finely chopped onion and garlic in the remaining fat for 4–5 minutes, or until slightly golden, stirring occasionally.
3   Return the meat to the casserole, cover with beef stock and red wine and bring to the boil over a gentle heat. Reduce the heat, cover and simmer for 1 hour.
4   In a small bowl, blend the chilli seasoning and flour with a little of the casserole liquid. Add the mixture to the casserole, together with the bay leaves, cumin powder and dried oregano. Season to taste with salt and freshly ground black pepper. Stir to blend in the seasonings and simmer gently for 1 hour, or until the meat is tender.
5   Adjust the seasoning, if necessary, and transfer to a heated serving dish. Garnish with bay leaves and strips of chilli, if wished. Serve with Mexican beans and Saffron rice.

● Mexican chilli seasoning is traditional for this dish; it is a strong but pleasant blend of spices. Do not confuse it with powdered chillies. They are so hot and strong that more than one pinch will render the dish inedible to many people.

  2¾ hours   lager

Mexican beans

Serves 4
250 g /8 oz red kidney beans, soaked overnight
1 Spanish onion, finely chopped
1 garlic clove, finely chopped
150 ml /5 fl oz beef stock, home-made or from a cube
25 g /1 oz butter
10 ml /2 tsp flour
1.5 ml /¼ tsp cumin powder
15 ml /1 tbls Mexican chilli seasoning
1 bouquet garni, made with 2 sprigs of thyme, 1 celery stick and
1 bay leaf
salt and freshly ground black pepper
lemon slices and flat-leaved parsley, to garnish
For the Saffron rice
850 ml /1½ pt chicken stock, home-made or from a cube
2.5 ml /½ tsp powdered saffron
90 ml /6 tbls dry white wine
350 g /12 oz long-grain rice
freshly ground black pepper

1   Drain the beans and place them in a large saucepan. Stir in the finely chopped onion and garlic and cover with 600 ml /1 pt water. Bring to the boil, boil hard for ten minutes, then reduce the heat, cover and simmer for 1 hour, or until the beans are tender but still whole. Drain well.
2   Put the beef stock in a clean saucepan and bring to the boil. In a small bowl, cream the butter and flour to a smooth paste. Add the cumin powder and the Mexican chilli seasoning and blend well. Add the paste to the stock very gradually, stirring well. When it is well blended, add the drained beans and the bouquet garni.
3   Season to taste with salt and freshly ground black pepper, bring to a simmer and cook, covered, for 45 minutes, or until the sauce is smooth and rich, stirring occasionally.
4   Meanwhile, make the Saffron rice. Heat the chicken stock in a large saucepan. Mix the saffron with the dry white wine and add to the stock. Add the rice and season with freshly ground black pepper.
5   Cover the pan and simmer for 20 minutes until the liquid is absorbed and the rice is tender.
6   Remove the bouquet garni from the kidney beans. Transfer the Saffron rice to a heated serving dish and spoon the kidney beans on top. Serve garnished with lemon slices and flat-leaved parsley.

 soaking the beans overnight, then 2 hours

Lettuce, watercress and orange salad

Serves 4
1 round lettuce
1 bunch of watercress
2 oranges
15–30 ml /1–2 tbls lemon juice
90 ml /6 tbls olive oil
salt and freshly ground black pepper
30 ml /2 tbls finely chopped fresh parsley

1 Wash the lettuce. Pat each leaf dry with a clean tea-towel or absorbent paper. Roll in a clean dry cloth and chill in the vegetable compartment of your refrigerator until needed.
2 Wash the watercress, trimming off the stalks and discarding any damaged leaves. Wrap in a clean tea-towel and chill in the vegetable compartment of your refrigerator until needed.
3 With a sharp knife, peel the oranges, slicing off the pith together with the skin, and catching the juices in a small bowl. Cut down on each side of the segments, lifting them out of the membranes. Squeeze the juice from the membranes into the bowl. Reserve the segments.
4 Combine the orange juices with the lemon juice and the olive oil and beat with a fork until the mixture emulsifies. Season to taste with salt and freshly ground black pepper.
5 Just before serving, toss the chilled lettuce and watercress leaves in the emulsified dressing until well coated. Dip the outer edge of the orange segments into the finely chopped parsley and arrange on the salad.

30 minutes,
plus chilling

Mexican custard tarts

Serves 4
8 × 6.5 cm /2½ in tart cases, made with shortcrust pastry, fully baked
2 egg yolks
60 ml /4 tbls icing sugar
5 ml /1 tsp cornflour
275 ml /10 fl oz milk
30 ml /2 tbls melted plain chocolate
1.5 ml /¼ tsp vanilla essence
2.5 ml /½ tsp grated orange zest
2.5 ml /½ tsp grated lemon zest
5–10 ml /1–2 tsp lemon juice
450 g /1 lb strawberries, hulled
30 ml /2 tbls Cointreau
450 g /1 lb raspberries
30 ml /2 tbls crème de cassis

1 In the top pan of a double boiler, off the heat, combine the egg yolks, icing sugar and cornflour and mix to a thick, smooth paste with a wooden spoon. Scald the milk in a separate pan.
2 Pour the scalded milk onto the egg yolk mixture in a thin stream, whisking vigorously. Cook over gently simmering water, stirring continuously, for 15–20 minutes, or until the custard becomes thick enough to coat the back of a wooden spoon. (A finger drawn across the back of the coated spoon should leave a clear trail.) Take the custard off the heat and keep stirring for 1–2 minutes while it cools a little.
3 Strain one-third of the custard into each of 3 serving bowls. Pour the melted chocolate into the first bowl and stir to blend. Blend the vanilla essence into the second bowl, and the grated orange and lemon zest and lemon juice into the third bowl. Cover the surface of the custard in each bowl with a piece of dampened greaseproof paper and chill.
4 Meanwhile, place the prepared strawberries in a small bowl and pour over the Cointreau. Mix lightly and chill. Place the raspberries in a separate small bowl and pour over the crème de cassis. Mix very lightly and chill.
5 When ready to serve, arrange the strawberries and raspberries in tall glass containers. Serve with the tart cases and the flavoured custards, leaving the guests to choose the fruit and filling of their choice.

making the tart cases,
then 50 minutes, plus chilling

Poultry & Game

PACKED WITH VARIETY!

Chilled Spanish soup

*Chicken with cream
and calvados*

Green peas with cucumber

Saffron pilaff

Apricot delight

Wine: a claret

Plan-ahead timetable

On the day before the meal
Chilled Spanish soup: make and chill the chicken stock, if making.
Saffron pilaff: make and chill the chicken stock, if making.
Apricot delight: make and freeze.

Three and a half hours before the meal
Chilled Spanish soup: make and chill the soup. Prepare and chill the side vegetables. Prepare the garlic croûtons.
Chicken with cream and calvados: cut, season, and set aside.

One and a quarter hours before the meal
Chicken with cream and calvados: brown, flame, then cook the chicken. Sauté the mushrooms. Prepare the *beurre manié*.
Green peas with cucumber: prepare the cucumber.

Thirty-five minutes before the meal
Saffron pilaff: sauté the onion and rice and then cook the rice.

Spark your appetite and sharpen your taste buds with Chilled Spanish soup. A purée of tomatoes and cucumber flavoured with garlic, lemon and parsley, it is served with garlic croûtons and bowls of finely chopped vegetables and hard-boiled eggs.

Chicken with cream and calvados is a dish in the tradition of Normandy. Butter and cream feature prominently in many of the regional dishes and this casserole of chicken cooked in thick cream is typical. Calvados, the delicious apple brandy of Normandy, also features in many of the region's specialities, both sweet and savoury. In my recipe, it serves to spike the richness of the sauce.

The French name of this dish is *Poulet François Premier*, to commemorate one of the great kings of the French Renaissance. Like many other aristocrats of the XVth and XVIth century, he was a patron of the arts, ranging from painting and sculpture to *l'art de la cuisine* — the art of cooking.

This is a rich chicken dish which is best complemented by a simple vegetable accompaniment. The Green peas with cucumber are cooked in chicken stock which has finely shredded mint added to it. The result is a tangy, piquant and refreshing dish. The other accompaniment that I have chosen is light and fluffy Saffron pilaff which will blend with the creamy chicken sauce to perfection. In addition to adding flavour, the saffron will turn the rice a wonderful bright yellow colour.

Finally, bring out the Apricot delight! Fresh apricots, puréed and combined with whisked egg whites and sugar, are frozen to a smooth, delicate ice. It is a fitting choice after a rich main course because it has no fat content and is therefore light. However, this absence of fat means that large ice crystals will form and you will need to beat the mixture well during freezing to keep the texture smooth.

To go with the meal, I suggest a claret. The really good ones tend to be expensive, of course, but enjoyable ones at lower prices are available, including claret-style wines.

Just before the meal

Chicken with cream and calvados: add the sautéed mushrooms to the chicken.

Green peas with cucumber: bring the water to the boil, add the stock cube and cook the vegetables.

Between the first and the main course

Chicken with cream and calvados: transfer the chicken to a serving dish. Complete the cooking of the sauce and serve.

Green peas with cucumber: transfer to a serving dish. Adjust the seasoning and serve.

Saffron pilaff: adjust the seasoning and transfer the rice to a serving dish. Garnish it and serve.

Apricot delight: transfer to the main part of the refrigerator to soften it a little.

Between the main course and the dessert

Apricot delight: remove from the refrigerator; scoop or spoon it into individual dishes, decorate and serve.

Chilled Spanish soup

Serves 4–6

2 slices of white bread
8 large tomatoes, blanched, skinned, seeded and diced
1 cucumber, peeled and chopped
850 ml /1½ pt chicken stock, home-made or from a cube
30 ml /2 tbls olive oil
30 ml /2 tbls lemon juice
2 small garlic cloves, finely chopped
60 ml /4 tbls finely chopped fresh parsley
salt and freshly ground black pepper
To serve
1 garlic clove
4 rounds of French bread
25 g /1 oz butter
1 green pepper, seeded and chopped
4 spring onions, finely chopped
2 hard-boiled eggs, finely chopped
7.5 cm /3 in piece of cucumber, peeled and chopped

1 Cut the crusts from the white bread and soak the bread in cold water.

2 In a large bowl, combine half the diced tomato flesh, the chopped cucumber, chicken stock, olive oil, lemon juice and finely chopped garlic, parsley and the soaked bread. Season this with salt and freshly ground black pepper to taste.

3 Purée the mixture in a blender. Adjust the seasoning, pour the soup into a tureen and chill.

4 To make the garlic croûtons, cut the garlic clove in half and rub each round of French bread on both sides with the cut side of the garlic clove. Sauté the bread in the butter until it is golden on both sides. Rub both sides again with the cut garlic clove.

5 Serve the chilled soup in individual bowls, garnishing each serving with a garlic croûton. Accompany the soup with small bowls of finely chopped pepper and spring onions, the remaining diced tomatoes, the chopped cucumber and chopped hard-boiled eggs.

● This lovely chilled soup is a variation of *gazpacho*, the famous iced soup of southern Spain.

30 minutes, plus chilling

Chicken with cream and calvados

Serves 4

1.4 kg /3 lb oven-ready chicken
salt and black pepper
25 g /1 oz butter
30 ml /2 tbls olive oil
60 ml /4 tbls calvados
150 ml /5 fl oz chicken stock,
  home-made or from a cube
275 ml /10 fl oz thick cream
bouquet garni
225 g /8 oz large, flat
  mushrooms
beurre manié, made by mashing
  together to a smooth paste
12.5 g /½ oz butter and
15 ml /1 tbls flour

1 Cut the chicken into 4 serving portions. Season them with freshly
ground black pepper and then leave them to come to room
temperature. Next, season them with salt.
2 In a frying-pan large enough to take the chicken portions in one
layer, heat the butter and olive oil. When the foaming subsides, lay the
chicken portions side by side in the hot fat and cook them over a high
heat for 3 minutes on each side, or until browned. Transfer the
browned chicken portions to a flameproof casserole large enough to
take them in one layer, reserving the fats in the frying-pan.
3 Heat the calvados in a metal ladle and ignite it with a lighted taper,
standing well back. Carefully pour the ignited calvados over the
chicken portions and allow the flames to die out.
4 Pour in the chicken stock and thick cream and then add the bouquet
garni. Bring the ingredients to a simmer, cover and simmer for 50–60
minutes, or until tender.
5 Meanwhile, reheat the fats in the frying-pan. Wipe the mushrooms
with a damp cloth and quarter them. Add the quartered mushrooms to
the hot fats and cook over a high heat for 3 minutes, or until browned,
tossing with a spatula.
6 Add the sautéed mushrooms to the chicken portions about
10 minutes before the chicken is cooked, pushing them between the
chicken portions to cover them with liquid.
7 Remove the bouquet garni. With a slotted spoon, transfer the
chicken to a heated, shallow serving dish and then arrange the
mushrooms over the chicken portions. Bring the remaining liquid to
the boil and add the *beurre manié*, a little at a time, whisking
vigorously to prevent lumps from forming. Boil for 1 minute. Adjust
the seasoning and pour it over the chicken and mushrooms and serve
immediately.

 bringing the chicken to room temperature,
then 1 hour 20 minutes

 a claret

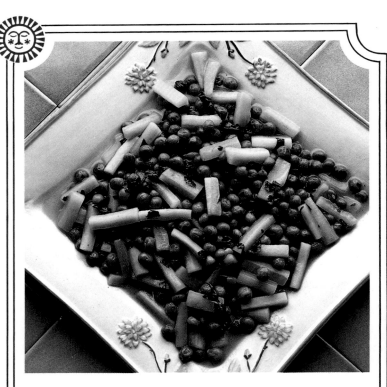

Green peas with cucumber

Serves 4

1 large cucumber
½ chicken stock cube
225 g /8 oz frozen peas
50 g /2 oz butter
fresh mint leaves, finely shredded
5 ml /1 tsp sugar
salt and freshly ground black pepper

1 Peel the cucumber and cut it lengthways down the middle into
2 long pieces. Remove the seeds with a teaspoon and cut each
cucumber half into 25 mm /1 in lengths. Cut each length into
6 × 25 mm /1 in long fingers.
2 In a heavy-based saucepan, bring 150 ml /5 fl oz water to the boil.
Stir in the chicken stock cube and dissolve. Add the cucumber fingers
and the frozen peas and bring them to the boil.
3 Stir in the butter, the finely shredded mint leaves and the sugar.
Season to taste with salt and freshly ground black pepper. Cover and
reduce the heat to a simmer. Simmer the vegetables gently for 3–5
minutes, or until they are tender.
4 Transfer the vegetables and the cooking liquor to a heated serving
dish. Adjust the seasoning and serve immediately.

● Fresh peas can also be used for this recipe, but they will need to be
cooked for a longer time.

20–25 minutes

Saffron pilaff

Serves 4

700 ml /1¼ pt well-flavoured chicken stock, home-made or from a
*   cube*
1.5 ml /¼ tsp saffron strands
40 g /1½ oz butter
½ Spanish onion, finely chopped
225 g /8 oz long-grain rice
salt and freshly ground black pepper
flat-leaved parsley, to garnish

1 Heat a little of the stock and soak the saffron strands in it. In a
heavy-based saucepan, melt the butter. Add the finely chopped onion
and cook it over a moderate heat for 7–10 minutes, or until it is soft
but not coloured, stirring occasionally with a wooden spoon.
2 Stir in the rice and cook it for 2–3 minutes, or until the grains have
taken on colour.
3 Meanwhile, heat the rest of the stock in a saucepan. Stir the saffron
strands and their soaking liquid into the rice and then add the stock.
Bring this to the boil. Season to taste with salt and freshly ground black
pepper. Reduce the heat, cover and simmer for about 18 minutes, or
until the rice is tender and has absorbed the liquid, stirring
occasionally.
4 Adjust the seasoning and transfer the rice to a heated serving
dish. Garnish it with a sprig of flat-leaved parsley and serve
immediately.

35–40 minutes

Apricot delight

Serves 4

175 g /6 oz sugar
100 g /4 oz fresh apricots, stoned and coarsely chopped
30 ml /2 tbls lemon juice
1 egg white
25 g /1 oz caster sugar
2 black grapes, halved and seeded, to garnish

1 If using the freezer compartment of your refrigerator, turn it down
to its lowest temperature (the highest setting) about 1 hour before you
make the apricot delight.
2 In a saucepan, stir the sugar and 125 ml /4 fl oz water over a gentle
heat until the sugar is dissolved. Bring to the boil and boil for
5 minutes, without stirring. Remove the syrup from the heat and leave
it to cool.
3 Place the chopped apricots in a blender with the lemon juice and
blend until smooth. Sieve the purée, using a wooden spoon to push the
pulp through the sieve. Add the cooled syrup to the sieved apricot
purée and stir until well blended.
4 In a bowl, whisk the egg white until soft peaks form. Gradually add
the caster sugar, again whisking until stiff peaks form. With a large
metal spoon, fold the meringue mixture into the apricot mixture. Pour
it into a shallow freezer-proof container and put it in the freezer
compartment of your refrigerator until the mixture is frozen to a depth
of 25 mm /1 in around the sides of the container.
5 Turn the apricot delight into a large bowl and whisk it with a fork
or wire whisk for 1–2 minutes until it is smooth. Return it to the
freezer and freeze again until it is firm.
6 Fifteen minutes before serving, transfer the apricot delight to the
main part of the refrigerator to soften it slightly.
7 When ready to serve, spoon or scoop the apricot delight into glass
dishes. Decorate each portion with a halved black grape and serve
immediately.

30 minutes,
   plus cooling and freezing

TURNING CARTWHEELS

Marinated tomato and onion salad

Fried chicken and spinach

Celery batons in pepper rings

Potatoes Anna

Latticed apple and lemon tart

Wine: white Rioja

The beauty of this Mediterranean-style meal is that many of the dishes need little preparation and can be made well ahead. Even the more complicated main course can be prepared in stages, needing only quick cooking at the last minute.

Marinated tomato and onion salad is beautifully quick and simple to prepare, but the flavour will, I'm sure, remind many readers of their last holiday in the sun. Combine the ingredients an hour before the meal and it will be all ready to serve to your guests without any extra fuss. Serve with French bread to mop up the delicious dressing.

My main course is Fried chicken and spinach. This dish is made with tender young chicken breasts simmered in white wine and stock, cooled, coated in bechamel sauce, chilled and then dipped in egg and breadcrumbs before deep frying. The chicken and the sauce can be made ahead and left to cool, needing only last-minute deep frying for the chicken, and the spinach purée to be heated through. The creaminess of the purée contrasts with the crunchy fried chicken to give a mouth-watering result.

The accompaniments to this eye-catching centre dish are also quick and easy to prepare. Celery batons in pepper rings speak for themselves — marinated in a tasty dressing the celery batons are secured in a ring of green pepper to make attractive individual servings. Potatoes Anna are an unusual way to serve potatoes — the recipe I use here is the classic version of this dish.

Finish the meal with the sweet and tangy mixture of Latticed apple and lemon tart — serve it with a jug of thick cream for a real treat.

For the wine I have chosen a white Rioja, in keeping with the feel of the meal. Rioja is a mountainous region of northern Spain which produces cheerful, inexpensive wines which are a pleasure to drink.

Plan-ahead timetable

On the day before the meal
Latticed apple and lemon tart: half-bake the pastry case and store it in an airtight container. Chill pastry trimmings in the refrigerator.

On the morning of the meal
Fried chicken and spinach: cook the chicken, make the bechamel sauce and cool. Coat the chicken with the sauce and cook and purée the spinach. Refrigerate both.
Latticed apple and lemon tart: add the apple filling and lattice to the tart and bake.

One and a half hours before the meal
Potatoes Anna: prepare the potatoes, slice, cover with water and reserve.

One and a quarter hours before the meal
Marinated tomato and onion salad: prepare the tomatoes and onions. Mix the dressing, then add it to the tomatoes and onions and marinate in the refrigerator.

Celery batons in pepper rings: blanch the celery, make the dressing and marinate.

Thirty minutes before the meal
Potatoes Anna: assemble, cook and transfer to the oven.
Fried chicken and spinach: breadcrumb the chicken breasts and then reserve them.

Just before the meal
Celery batons in pepper rings: assemble carefully and pour some dressing over them.

Between the first and the main course
Fried chicken and spinach: fry the chicken breasts. Reheat the spinach purée, assemble carefully, garnish and then serve immediately.
Latticed apple and lemon tart: reheat in a low oven, if the tart is to be served warm.

Between the main course and the dessert
Latticed apple and lemon tart: remove from the oven, and serve with thick cream, if wished.

Marinated tomato and onion salad

Serves 6
450 g /1 lb tomatoes
2 button onions, peeled
salt and freshly ground black pepper
For the dressing
90 ml /6 tbls olive oil
30 ml /2 tbls wine vinegar
5 ml /1 tsp Dijon mustard
5 ml /1 tsp tomato purée
2.5 ml /¹/₂ tsp caster sugar
a pinch of mild chilli seasoning
salt and freshly ground black pepper
French bread, to serve

1 Put the tomatoes in a bowl, cover with boiling water and leave for about 30 seconds. Drain and peel off the skins.
2 Slice the skinned tomatoes and the peeled button onions thinly. Separate the onion slices into rings. Arrange half the sliced tomatoes in a layer at the bottom of a serving dish. Season with salt and freshly ground black pepper. Sprinkle with half the sliced onions. Repeat with the remaining tomato slices and onion slices.
3 In a bowl, combine the olive oil, wine vinegar, Dijon mustard, tomato purée, caster sugar, pinch of chilli seasoning and salt and freshly ground black pepper to taste. Beat with a wooden spoon until the mixture emulsifies and then pour it over the tomato and onion layers.
4 Transfer the salad to the refrigerator and leave it to marinate for about 1 hour. Serve chilled with crusty French bread.

10 minutes, plus marinating

Fried chicken and spinach

Serves 6

6 chicken breasts
salt and ground black pepper
2 leeks, finely chopped
4 sprigs of parsley
1 bay leaf
175 ml /6 fl oz dry white wine
150 ml /5 fl oz chicken stock
4 × bechamel sauce (see
   recipe for Stuffed tomato
   soufflés page 17) made with
   30 ml /2 tbls extra of butter
   and flour

oil, for deep frying
120 ml /8 tbls seasoned flour
2 eggs, beaten
50 g /2 oz fresh white
   breadcrumbs
bouquet of flat-leaved parsley, to
   garnish
For the spinach purée
1 kg /2 lb spinach
50 g /2 oz butter
salt
freshly ground black pepper

1   Heat the oven to 200C /400F /gas 6.
2   Cut the wings from the chicken breasts if necessary and remove the skin and any bones. Season generously with salt and pepper.
3   In an ovenproof dish large enough to take the chicken breasts in one layer, combine the finely chopped leeks, sprigs of parsley, bay leaf, white wine and chicken stock. Add the chicken breasts, cover and cook for 50–60 minutes, turning once. Cool in the liquid.
4   Meanwhile, make the bechamel sauce. Leave it to become cool.
5   Reserving 60 ml /4 tbls cooking liquid, lay the chicken breasts on a wire rack over a baking tray. Coat with bechamel sauce. Chill.
6   Wash the spinach in several changes of cold water. Melt the butter in a heavy-based saucepan, add the spinach and 60 ml /4 tbls chicken liquid. Season, then cook over a high heat for 5 minutes or until the spinach is tender, stirring. Drain, purée the spinach or pass through a vegetable mill. Put the purée in the top pan of a double boiler with 90 ml /6 tbls of the bechamel sauce that has dropped from the chicken portions. Season and keep warm.
7   Heat the oil in a deep-fat frier to 190C /375F.
8   Place the seasoned flour on a plate, the beaten eggs in a shallow dish and the breadcrumbs in a bowl. Toss each bechamel-coated chicken breast in flour, shaking off the excess. Dip them in beaten egg to cover and toss in breadcrumbs, firmly patting on the coating.
9   Deep fry in two batches for 2 minutes, or until golden brown.
10   Spread the spinach purée on a flat dish. Place the chicken breasts on top, garnish with parsley and serve.

 2 hours, plus cooling and chilling

 white Rioja

Celery batons in pepper rings

Serves 6

1 large head of celery
salt
135 ml /9 tbls olive oil
45 ml /3 tbls wine vinegar
7.5 ml /1½ tsp Dijon mustard
coarse salt and freshly ground black pepper
6 small green pepper rings

1   Trim and wash the celery and cut the celery sticks into 4 cm × 3 mm /1½ × ⅛ in batons. Blanch them in a saucepan of boiling salted water for 10 minutes, or until tender. Drain and rinse under cold running water and drain again.
2   In a bowl, combine the olive oil, wine vinegar and Dijon mustard with coarse salt and freshly ground black pepper to taste. Beat with a fork until the mixture emulsifies. Add the blanched and drained celery batons, toss and leave to marinate for 1 hour.
3   Drain the celery batons and reserve the marinade. Divide the celery batons into 6 bundles. Put each bundle through a green pepper ring and arrange in a serving dish. Pour a little of the reserved dressing over the bundles. Serve immediately.

30 minutes,
plus marinating

Potatoes Anna

Serves 6
700 g /1½ lb even-sized floury potatoes
75 g /3 oz butter
salt and freshly ground black pepper
30 ml /2 tbls finely chopped fresh parsley

1 Peel or scrape the potatoes, then cut into very thin slices — no more than 3 mm /⅛ in thick. Heat the oven to 200C /400F /gas 6.
2 Select a cast-iron pan, about 20–23 cm /8–9 in in diameter and 7.5–10 cm /3–4 in deep, with rounded or sloping sides and a well-fitting lid. (A heavy frying-pan with the same dimensions can be used.) Place half the butter in the pan and allow it to melt over a moderate heat. When the butter is foaming, but not brown, remove the pan from the heat.
3 Starting at the centre, arrange a layer of slightly overlapping potato slices in a spiral pattern over the base of the pan and up the sides. Take care to arrange this first layer neatly as the dish is turned out for serving. Season to taste with salt and freshly ground black pepper and dot with a little of the remaining butter.
4 Continue to layer the potatoes in the pan until all the slices are used up. Season to taste and dot with butter every two layers, but make sure to reserve some butter for the final layer. Dot the last layer of potatoes with the reserved butter.
5 Set the pan over a moderate heat and cook for 10 minutes, shaking the pan gently to prevent the potatoes sticking to the base. Then cover the pan with a well-fitting lid and bake in the oven for 30 minutes, or until the potatoes are tender when pierced with a knife. Halfway through the baking time, remove the lid to allow the potatoes to crisp slightly and steam to escape.
6 To serve, turn out the potato 'cake' onto a heated serving dish. If the top of the 'cake' is a little over-brown or has stuck slightly, a sprinkling of finely chopped parsley will disguise any problems.

● The classic version of Potatoes Anna uses no grated onion or cheese, but either or both may be included for variety. Use ½ a Spanish onion, grated, and /or 45 ml /3 tbls freshly grated Parmesan cheese; sprinkle between the layers of potato, but not over the final layer. Cook and bake as above.
● If necessary, this dish can be baked at a lower oven temperature — but allow a longer cooking time.

Latticed apple and lemon tart

Serves 6
350 g /12 oz made-weight shortcrust pastry, defrosted if frozen
4 tart dessert apples
1 egg
60 ml /4 tbls caster sugar
60 ml /4 tbls melted butter
zest and juice of 1 lemon
1 egg yolk, beaten
jug of thick cream, to serve (optional)

1 Roll the pastry out 3–6 mm /⅛–¼ in thick. Lift it on the rolling pin over a 20 cm /8 in loose-bottomed tart tin.
2 Press the pastry into the tin from the base outwards. Do not stretch it or it will shrink back later. Trim away the extra pastry by rolling it over the flan case with the pin. Reserve the trimmings. Prick the base with a fork, then chill for 30 minutes.
3 Heat the oven and a baking sheet to 200C /400F /gas 6. Line the pastry case with foil and fill with dried beans. Bake on the heated baking sheet for 10 minutes.
4 Turn down the oven to 180C /350F /gas 4. Remove the foil and beans and bake the pastry case for a further 8–10 minutes.
5 Remove the half-baked pastry case from the oven and turn up the oven to 190C /375F /gas 5.
6 Roll out the reserved trimmings into an oblong, 3 mm /⅛ in thick, and cut it lengthways into 6 mm /¼ in strips for the lattice.
7 Peel, quarter and core the apples. Slice each quarter thinly. Arrange the slices in overlapping circles in the prepared pastry case until all the apples are used.
8 In a bowl, beat the egg and caster sugar until well blended. Stir in the melted butter and zest and juice of 1 lemon. Pour the mixture over the apple slices.
9 Brush the rim of the pastry with beaten egg yolk. Lay a lattice of pastry strips across the tart, cutting off the excess length and pushing the ends down firmly on the rim. Brush egg yolk over the lattice and bake in the oven for 25–30 minutes, or until the lattice is golden and the apples are tender. Leave to cool slightly.
10 Transfer the slightly cooled tart to a serving plate and serve warm or cold, with a jug of thick cream, if wished.

 1 hour

 1¼ hours, plus chilling

A SPECIAL DINNER FOR EIGHT

Pain de sole

Braised duck in brandy

Potatoes with parsley butter

Boiled spinach with nutmeg

Lemon sorbet

Wine: Côte de Rôtie

Plan-ahead timetable

On the day before the meal
Lemon sorbet: make the sorbet and keep it in the freezer compartment of the refrigerator.
Braised duck in brandy: cut the duck into serving pieces and marinate in the refrigerator.

On the morning of the meal
Braised duck in brandy: cook and leave to cool in the casserole.
Pain de sole: prepare the terrine, make the fish purée and the herb forcemeat, layer into the terrine with the fillets and leave, covered, in the refrigerator.

Four hours before the meal
Pain de sole: Remove from the refrigerator; leave at room temperature.
Boiled spinach with nutmeg: wash the spinach, discard any blemished leaves and the stems.

One and three quarter hours before the meal
Pain de sole: put in a bain-marie with boiling water and cook.
Potatoes with parsley butter: peel the potatoes and scoop into balls; keep covered in water..

Today nearly everyone cooks and nearly everyone loves to entertain. Eating well holds a fascination for all of us — a fact that is very much in evidence from the top restaurants to private homes. Food is now as suitable a subject for heated discussions as politics, clothes and bestsellers. If you want your friends to enthuse about the food you serve when you entertain, here is a gourmet dinner party menu for eight that is rich in flavour and contrasts. It will certainly give your friends something to talk about. It is not an inexpensive dinner — nor is it one that can be prepared in just a few minutes, but with careful planning, following my timetable, it need not be too daunting.

This is a dinner that is meant for cooks who really like to cook and for guests who know how to appreciate the food served to them. But, in its way, it is an extremely practical dinner, too. The two cooked courses are easy to serve and each can be prepared in advance. The Pain de sole (a delicate fish loaf) can be made in the morning and refrigerated until two hours before it is popped into the oven. The Braised duck in brandy — a rich stew of tender duckling simmered in brandy and wine and garnished with button mushrooms and onions — can be marinated overnight, cooked in the morning and then reheated while your guests are enjoying their pre-dinner drinks.

Serve the deliciously light Pain de sole in thick slices as a hot first course. The duck stew is excellent served with boiled rice or puréed potatoes, but for this menu I have chosen Potatoes with parsley butter. It takes a little extra effort to cut out the potato shapes but the finished dish is well worth while. Lightly cooked spinach tossed in butter and seasoned with nutmeg is the perfect choice for the rich main course. The duck is good, too, when followed by a ripe Camembert or Brie, accompanied perhaps with two or three Philadelphia cream cheeses quartered and rolled in cumin seeds. To finish the meal on a sharp note, try a home-made Lemon sorbet, scooped out and piled into a serving dish garnished with shiny (non-toxic!) green leaves.

One hour before the meal
Boiled spinach with nutmeg: cook the spinach, drain and cool.

Forty-five minutes before the meal
Braised duck in brandy: cook the onions and mushrooms.

Thirty minutes before the meal
Braised duck in brandy: heat the duck in the casserole.
Potatoes with parsley butter: cook the potatoes.
Lemon sorbet: put the sorbet in the main part of the refrigerator.

Twenty minutes before the meal
Boiled spinach with nutmeg: heat the spinach and butter.
Potatoes with parsley butter: make the parsley butter; combine with the potatoes and keep warm.
Pain de sole: remove the fish loaf from the oven. Keep warm and unmould just before serving.

Between the first and the main course
Braised duck in brandy: remove the duck from the casserole, add the consommé and tomato purée to the liquid and thicken.
Pour the sauce over the duck, garnish and serve.

Between the main course and the dessert
Lemon sorbet: scoop the sorbet into balls and garnish.

Pain de sole

Serves 8

550 g /1¼ lb fillets of lemon sole; about 10 fillets
3 egg whites
salt and freshly ground pepper
a pinch of cayenne pepper
425 ml /15 fl oz thick cream
2–3 sprigs of tarragon
100–175 g /4–6 oz pork fat in thin strips

For the herb forcemeat
3 eggs
175 g /6 oz fresh white breadcrumbs
60 ml /4 tbls finely chopped fresh parsley
30 ml /2 tbls finely chopped fresh tarragon
15 ml /1 tbls finely snipped chives

1 Set aside 4 good-sized fillets of sole and mince the remainder of the fish. Stir two unbeaten egg whites into the minced fish and rub this mixture through a fine sieve into a bowl.

2 Set the bowl in a larger bowl containing ice cubes. Work the mixture, adding salt, black pepper and cayenne. When the fish stiffens, slowly fold in 275 ml /10 fl oz of the cream. Remove from the ice, cover the bowl and leave at the bottom of the refrigerator until needed.

3 For the herb forcemeat, beat the whole eggs lightly and whisk in the remaining cream. Add the breadcrumbs, parsley, tarragon and snipped chives. Mix well and season to taste.

4 Beat the remaining egg white until foamy. Season the reserved fillets of sole with salt and freshly ground black pepper.

5 Arrange 2 or 3 sprigs of tarragon on the base of a 1.7 L /3 pt terrine. Line the base and the sides with the strips of pork fat, making sure that they overlap the edges.

6 Spread the base and sides of the terrine with two-thirds of the fish purée. Brush with the egg white and place two fillets on the base. Brush the fillets with egg white and cover with half of the forcemeat. Brush with the egg white; lay the remaining fillets on top and brush them also. Cover with the remaining forcemeat, brush with egg white, then fill the terrine with the remaining fish purée. Fold over the overlapping pork fat and refrigerate until needed.

7 Heat the oven to 150C /300F /gas 2. Place the terrine in a pan with boiling water to come a third of the way up its sides. Bake for 1½ hours or until a sharp skewer pushed through the centre and held there for a few seconds feels hot on the palm of your hand.

8 Turn the pain de sole out onto a heated serving dish and cut into thick slices. Serve immediately.

● This dish is good served with Mousseline-hollandaise sauce.

 1¼ hours, then 1½ hours cooking

Braised duck in brandy

Serves 8

2 × 2 kg /4½ lb oven-ready
   ducks
salt and freshly ground pepper
2 bay leaves
2.5 ml /½ tsp dried thyme
2 celery sticks, finely chopped
2 carrots, sliced 5 mm /¼ in thick
2 large Spanish onions, chopped
125 ml /4 fl oz brandy
700 ml /1¼ pt dry wine
225 g /8 oz bacon in one piece
50 g /2 oz flour

bouquet garni
2 garlic cloves, finely chopped
24 button onions
75 g /3 oz butter
30 ml /2 tbls caster sugar
350 g /12 oz button mushrooms
425 ml /15 fl oz canned consommé
   reduced to 15–30 ml /1–2 tbls
15–30 ml /1–2 tbls tomato purée
a pinch of cayenne pepper
15–30 ml /1–2 tbls snipped
   chives

1 Cut each duck into 4. Place in a large bowl. Season and add the bay
leaves, thyme, celery, carrots, onions, brandy and wine. Leave to
marinate for at least 2 hours or overnight.
2 Remove the duck and dry; reserve the marinade. Cut the bacon into
small fingers and sauté it in its own fat until golden. Transfer the
bacon to a large flameproof casserole.
3 Coat the duck pieces in 30 ml /2 tbls of the flour. Brown the duck
in the fat remaining in the pan and add it to the casserole with the pan
juices and fat. Cover, cook over a low heat for 15 minutes.
4 Pour off the fat and add the reserved marinade, bouquet garni and
garlic to the casserole. Bring to the boil, then simmer gently, covered,
for ¾–1 hour, or until the duck is tender.
5 Meanwhile, put the onions in a saucepan with 50 ml /2 fl oz water,
25 g /1 oz of the butter and the sugar; season to taste. Bring to the boil,
then simmer, shaking the pan occasionally, until the liquid has boiled
away and the onions are caramelized. Keep hot.
6 Put the mushrooms in a pan with 25 g /1 oz of the butter and toss
over a gentle heat until tender. Keep them hot.
7 Transfer the duck to a heated serving dish, strain the sauce and
skim off any fat. Add the consommé and tomato purée; mix well.
8 Work the remaining flour and butter to form a *beurre manié* and add
in tiny pieces to the simmering sauce. Cook for 2–3 minutes, stirring,
until the sauce is smooth and thickened. Adjust the seasoning and add
the cayenne pepper. Pour the sauce over the duck, garnish with the
onions, mushrooms and chives and serve.

  overnight marinating,
then 1¾ hours   Côte Rotie

Potatoes with parsley butter

Serves 8

1.8 kg /4 lb potatoes
salt
50 g /2 oz butter, melted
30 ml /2 tbls finely chopped fresh parsley
2.5 ml /½ tsp lemon juice

1 Peel the potatoes. Using a melon baller cut out as many perfect
potato balls as you can. Cook the potato balls in boiling salted water
until just tender — about 15 minutes. Drain them carefully.
2 Combine the hot melted butter with the finely chopped parsley and
the lemon juice.
3 Dress the potatoes with the hot parsley butter. Turn into a heated
serving dish and serve immediately.

● Great attention should be paid to the variety of potato you use in
this dish. If the potato balls are too floury or break up when being
tossed in the butter, the effect is spoilt. A waxy potato like Desirée is
ideal.
● Any bits of potato left over when you have made the potato balls
can be used to thicken a soup or make a purée. Keep them covered in
water until you use them or they will discolour.

 30 minutes

Boiled spinach with nutmeg

Serves 8
1.8 kg /4 lb spinach
50–75 g /2–3 oz butter
salt and freshly ground black pepper
freshly grated nutmeg

1 Wash the spinach carefully, leaf by leaf, to remove any specks of sand or grit. Discard any yellowed, pale or blemished leaves and pull away the stems. If they are tender they will snap off at the base of the leaf, but if they are tough the stem will rip along the whole length of the leaf.
2 Shake the leaves to get rid of any excess moisture and pack them into a very large saucepan. (For this amount of spinach it may be necessary to use 2 saucepans.) Turn the heat up fairly high; cover tightly and allow the spinach to cook in the water left clinging to the leaves. Do not add salt at this stage.
3 When you hear sizzling noises coming from the pan, cook for 1–2 minutes longer. Uncover the pan and turn over the leaves with a fork so that the uncooked layer on the top takes the place of the cooked leaves underneath. Cook for a further 1–2 minutes, then remove from the heat.
4 Drain the cooked spinach in a colander, pressing it firmly to extract any remaining moisture. If desired, chop the spinach using 2 round-bladed knives with the blades cutting across each other in a scissor-fashion.
5 Return the spinach to the dry pan, dress with the butter and season with salt, freshly ground black pepper and a little grated nutmeg to taste.
6 Stir over a low heat until the butter has melted and the spinach has heated through. Serve immediately.

25 minutes

Lemon sorbet

Serves 8
225 g /8 oz sugar
finely grated zest of 1 large lemon
275 ml /10 fl oz fresh lemon juice
1 egg white
8 shiny (non-toxic) leaves, to garnish

1 If you are using the freezing compartment of a refrigerator, turn the refrigerator down to its lowest temperature (the highest setting) about 1 hour before you start to make the sorbet.
2 Bring the sugar and 700 ml /1¼ pt water to the boil; boil for 5 minutes. Remove the syrup from the heat and add the grated lemon zest. Leave the syrup to stand until it is lukewarm.
3 Mix the lemon juice into the syrup, stir once and leave to cool completely.
4 When it is cold, strain it through a fine sieve into ice cube trays with the dividers removed, a loaf tin or a suitable container. Cover it and put it in the freezing compartment of the refrigerator. Leave until the sorbet mixture freezes to 25 mm /1 in thick around the sides of the container. This will take about 1 hour in ice cube trays, about 2½ hours in a loaf tin or polythene container.
5 Whisk the lemon sorbet with a fork or wire whisk to break up the ice particles and return, covered, to the freezer for 30 minutes.
6 Remove from the freezer and whisk with a fork or wire whisk until smooth, then whisk the egg white until stiff and fold in. (I do this in an electric food processor to incorporate air more quickly.) Return to the freezer, covered, until the sorbet is firm.
7 Thirty minutes before serving, transfer the sorbet to the ordinary chilling part of the refrigerator to soften slightly.
8 To serve, form the sorbet into 16 balls and pile them into a glass dish. Garnish with the shiny leaves.

● You will need 10 small lemons (or 7 large juicy lemons) to get 275 ml /10 fl oz lemon juice.

15 minutes, plus 3½–5 hours cooling and freezing, beating at intervals

MAKING THE MOST OF GAME

Grouse are the first game birds of the British shooting season. To make the most of this succulent bird, stuff it with a moist mixture of well-seasoned apple, orange and onion and top it with a protective cover of fat salt pork or unsmoked bacon. The cooking time varies according to the age and size of the grouse. Those available in the new season should be plump, so cook them for 30–35 minutes. The cooked bird should be pink and moist, never overcooked, or the meat will toughen.

The traditional accompaniment to roast grouse is a croûton of bread cut into a rectangle large enough to serve as a base for the grouse, then fried in clarified butter and olive oil. The grouse livers are sautéed, puréed, seasoned and then spread on the croûton to enhance its flavour.

When I am feeling affluent, I like to serve a whole grouse to each guest and the portions of the other courses on this menu are geared to this. However, if you prefer, a young bird can be split in two to serve half a grouse per person. Later in the season, when birds are larger, this is a must. Serve the grouse with rich Red cabbage-in-the-pot and Game chips, a traditional British garnish for game and the original wafer-thin fried potatoes.

Start the meal with Prawn and citrus salad — a pleasant, tangy taste of citrus fruit to prepare the taste buds for the richness of the grouse to follow. After the game, clean the palate with a Pear and watercress salad and follow this with an unusual Mixed fruit trifle. Bring the meal to a quiet finale with a selection of cheeses — Stilton, Cheddar, Blue Cheshire and Caerphilly, crisp celery and some grapes. **Note:** this is a classic roast game menu and as such any other game bird — or even venison — is interchangeable with the grouse.

Prawn and citrus salad

Roast grouse
Red cabbage-in-the-pot
Game chips
Pear and watercress salad

Mixed fruit trifle
English cheeseboard

Wine: Morey-St Denis

Plan-ahead timetable

On the morning of the meal
Mixed fruit trifle: combine the cake and custard and chill.
Poach the pear and chill.

Two hours before the meal
English cheeseboard: arrange the cheeses on the cheeseboard, cover them lightly and keep them in a cool place. Prepare the celery.
Roast grouse: make the stuffing, stuff, truss and bard.
Prawn and citrus salad: boil the prawns and leave them until cold. Make the vinaigrette and mayonnaise, if using.

One and a half hours before the meal
Prawn and citrus salad: prepare the grapefruit and oranges. Combine with the prawns and chill. Chill the bowls.
Pear and watercress salad: prepare the watercress and chill.

One hour before the meal
Game chips: peel and slice the potatoes and keep them in water.
Red cabbage-in-the-pot: assemble the ingredients and reserve.

Thirty minutes before the meal
Pear and watercress salad: make the julienne strips and dressing.
Roast grouse: make the croûtons and liver purée; keep warm.

Fifteen minutes before the meal
Roast grouse: put them in the oven to cook.
Red cabbage-in-the-pot: bring to the boil, then simmer.
Prawn and citrus salad: add the vinaigrette to the prawn mixture. Arrange in bowls and garnish.

Between the first and the main course
Game chips: heat the oil, fry the chips, drain and serve.
Pear and watercress salad: assemble the salad.
Roast grouse: discard the apple and orange mixture, spread the liver purée on the croûtons and serve the grouse.

Between the main course and the dessert
Mixed fruit trifle: top the trifle with cream and fruit.

Prawn and citrus salad

Serves 4
225 g /8 oz boiled shelled prawns, fresh if possible
60 ml /4 tbls finely chopped onion
60 ml /4 tbls finely chopped fresh parsley
20 ml /4 tsp lemon juice
60 ml /4 tbls olive oil
¼ crumbled chicken stock cube
salt and freshly ground black pepper
a pinch of cayenne pepper
2 large grapefruits
2 large oranges
275 ml /10 fl oz well-flavoured vinaigrette dressing (page 67)
For the garnish
lettuce leaves
60 ml /4 tbls thick mayonnaise, if wished (page 35)
black olives
tomato wedges

1   Put the prawns in a saucepan with the finely chopped onion, parsley, lemon juice, olive oil and crumbled chicken stock cube. Add salt and freshly ground black pepper and cayenne pepper to taste. Bring the ingredients to the boil, then remove them from the heat and leave them to become completely cold.
2   Put 4 glass bowls into the refrigerator to chill.
3   Meanwhile, use a sharp knife to peel all the rind and pith from the grapefruits and oranges. Cut down between the membranes to divide them into segments. Drain off any excess juice.
4   When the prawns are cold, drain them thoroughly. Combine them with the grapefruit and orange segments. Add the vinaigrette dressing and season the mixture with a little more salt, freshly ground black pepper and cayenne pepper.
5   Line each chilled glass bowl with lettuce leaves and divide the prawn and citrus mixture among them. Top each serving with 15 ml / 1 tbls mayonnaise, if wished, and garnish with black olives and tomato wedges. Serve very cold.

making the vinaigrette and mayonnaise, then 20 minutes, plus chilling

Roast grouse

Serves 4

4 young grouse, 350–450 g /
  12 oz–1 lb each, dressed
  weight, with livers
  reserved
1 red apple, cored
1 orange
1 small Spanish onion, chopped
salt
freshly ground black pepper

75 ml /5 tbls olive oil
8 thin slices of salt pork or
  unsmoked bacon
65 g /2½ oz butter
4 × 10 mm /½ in thick, large slices
  of bread, crusts removed
50 g /2 oz clarified butter
cayenne pepper (optional)
sprigs of watercress, to garnish

1　Heat the oven to 220C /425F /gas 7. Wipe the birds carefully, both inside and out, with a damp cloth. Reserve the livers.
2　Chop the apple and orange, zest and all, and put them in a bowl. Add the onion, season with salt and freshly ground black pepper, and moisten with 15 ml /1 tbls of the olive oil.
3　Pack the grouse cavities tightly with the orange and apple mixture. Secure the grouse cavities.
4　Rub the birds all over with black pepper. Bard the breast of each with 2 thin slices of salt pork or bacon, and tie into place. Butter a roasting tin with 15 g /½ oz of the butter and lay the grouse in it.
5　Roast the grouse for about 30–35 minutes, depending on their size. Ten minutes before the end of the cooking time, remove the barding fat to allow the birds to brown. Test to see if they are cooked by piercing the flesh between the leg and breast with a fine skewer; the juices should run slightly pink.
6　Meanwhile, before the grouse are ready, fry the bread in a mixture of the clarified butter and the remaining olive oil until crisp and golden brown on both sides. Drain well on absorbent paper. Place on a heated serving dish and keep warm.
7　In a small pan, sauté the grouse livers in 25 g /1 oz of the remaining butter for 2–3 minutes. Using a mortar and pestle or a blender, purée the livers, then work in the remaining butter. Season with salt and black pepper, or a pinch of cayenne pepper.
8　When ready to serve, remove the trussing. Discard the orange and apple mixture. Spread the croûtons with the liver mixture and place a grouse on each croûton. Garnish with sprigs of watercress and Game chips and serve.

● The timings and temperatures given here are for immature grouse, allowing 1 bird per person. A larger bird will feed 2 people and will need a longer roasting time if stuffed.

 1 hour　　　Morey-St Denis
or another burgundy

Red cabbage-in-the-pot

Serves 4

1 red cabbage, weighing about 500 g /1 lb
25 g /1 oz butter
225 g /8 oz cooking apples
175 g /6 oz onions
1 garlic clove, finely chopped
a large pinch of grated nutmeg
a large pinch of ground allspice
a large pinch of ground cinnamon
a large pinch of dried thyme
a large pinch of caraway seed
salt
freshly ground black pepper
5 ml /1 tsp grated orange zest
30 ml /2 tbls soft brown sugar
75 ml /5 tbls red wine
15 m /1 tbls wine vinegar

1　Remove any damaged outer leaves from the cabbage. Wash the cabbage, cut it into quarters and remove the central core. Shred the cabbage finely.
2　Melt the butter in a saucepan and add the cabbage. Cover the pan and cook for 5 minutes over a low heat. Peel and core the apples and cut them into slices. Slice the onions.
3　In a deep flameproof casserole, layer the cabbage, onion and apples. Season each layer with finely chopped garlic, the spices and herbs, the salt and freshly ground pepper to taste, and the grated orange zest. Sprinkle the brown sugar over the top, and add the wine and wine vinegar.
4　Bring the ingredients to the boil, then cover, reduce the heat and simmer for 20 minutes, or until tender but still crisp.

● If you find it more convenient, the casserole can be simmered in the oven, heated to 200C /400F /gas 6, for 20 minutes.

 45 minutes

Game chips

Serves 4
500 g /1 lb potatoes
oil, for deep frying
salt

1 Peel the potatoes and cut them into paper-thin slices, using a mandolin cutter if you have one.
2 Rinse the potato slices thoroughly under cold running water to rid them of their surface starch. Dry the potato slices individually with a clean cloth or absorbent paper immediately before frying.
3 Heat the oil in a deep-fat frier to 200C /400F — a cube of bread will turn brown in 40 seconds at this temperature. Deep fry the potato slices in batches. Do not overcrowd the pan — the oil should return almost immediately to its initial temperature as the potatoes should only need 1–2 minutes to become crisp and golden. Drain each batch on absorbent paper, sprinkle them with salt and keep them warm.
4 To serve, place the game chips on the serving dish with the game, or serve them separately in a bowl.

● If you want to prepare the chips some time before frying, keep the potato slices in a bowl of cold water to prevent discoloration.

Pear and watercress salad

Serves 4
1 bunch of watercress
½ celery stick
1 Comice or other dessert pear
For the vinaigrette dressing
30 ml /2 tbls wine vinegar
5 ml /1 tsp Dijon mustard
coarse salt
freshly ground black pepper
120 ml /8 tbls olive oil

1 Wash and trim the watercress, discarding any yellow or damaged leaves. Dry it thoroughly and wrap it in a damp tea-towel, then chill it in the refrigerator.
2 Cut the half celery stick into 4 cm /1½ in lengths, then, with a sharp knife, pare each piece lengthways into thin strips.
3 To make the vinaigrette dressing, combine the vinegar, mustard, a generous pinch of salt, and freshly ground black pepper to taste in a bowl. Beat in the olive oil with a whisk until the dressing thickens and emulsifies.
4 Just before serving, cut the pear into quarters and core them neatly. Cut each quarter into 6 slices. In a salad bowl, toss the watercress, pear slices and julienne strips of celery with the dressing. Arrange the salad decoratively so that some of the pear slices show through the watercress, with the celery on top. Serve immediately, otherwise the watercress will wilt.

● Serve this salad on small plates after the main course.

 30 minutes

 20 minutes

Mixed fruit trifle

Serves 4–6

400 g /14 oz canned peeled
* apricots, drained*
20 cm /8 in sponge layer cake
150 ml /5 fl oz Marsala
450–600 ml /³⁄₄–1 pt thick
* cream*
2.5 ml /¹⁄₂ tsp vanilla essence
60 ml /4 tbls caster sugar
2 kiwi fruit, peeled and sliced
2 red-skinned apples, thinly sliced,
* dipped in lemon juice*

1 medium-sized pear, poached in
* red wine and water,*
* to cover*
12 mint leaves
For the custard
30 ml /2 tbls cornflour
30 ml /2 tbls caster sugar
275 ml /10 fl oz milk
3 eggs, beaten
50 g /2 oz crumbled macaroon
* biscuits*

1 Purée the apricots in a blender. Cut the sponge cake into 2 layers. Sandwich the 2 layers together with half of the apricot purée. Cut the assembled cake into 2.5×5 cm /1×2 in pieces. Arrange the cake pieces in the bottom of a large glass serving dish. Pour the Marsala over the pieces and spread the remaining apricot purée over the top.
2 To make the custard, in a small bowl mix the cornflour and sugar to a smooth paste with 45 ml /3 tbls milk. Bring the remaining milk to the boil in the top part of a double boiler over direct heat. Pour the milk over the cornflour mixture and blend well. Return the mixture to the pan and cook in the double boiler over simmering water for about 10 minutes, stirring constantly with a wooden spoon, or until the mixture thickens.
3 Remove from the heat and gradually beat in the eggs. When well blended, cook gently over hot but not boiling water, stirring occasionally, for 10 minutes. Do not allow the mixture to boil or the custard will curdle. Stir in the crumbled macaroons and leave to soak for 15 minutes, or until soft. Beat well to incorporate the macaroons evenly and then leave until cold.
4 Pour the cold custard over the apricot purée and cake. Chill it in the refrigerator for at least 2 hours.
5 Just before serving, whisk the thick cream with the vanilla essence and the sugar until thick. Spread the cream over the custard. Place the kiwi fruit slices around the outer edge of the dish. Use the apple slices to form an inner circle, leaving a space in the middle of the cream for the pear. Place the poached pear in the centre and surround it with the mint leaves.

  1³⁄₄ hours,
plus 2 hours chilling time

English cheeseboard

Serve a selection of English cheeses, accompanied by dry unsalted biscuits, crisp celery, and grapes, if wished.

Stilton
One of England's famous cheeses, Stilton is sometimes called the world's most regal blue cheese. When properly ripened, its blue mould should be evenly distributed all over the surface in wide-branching veins; the background colour of a ripe Stilton is a rich cream, not an anaemic white. The best season for this richly-flavoured cheese in its home country is between November and April. It should be eaten within 6 weeks of purchase.

Cheddar
By far the most popular of cheeses, Cheddar is cream to soft gold in colour, close and buttery in texture and has a full, clean, nutty flavour. It tends to go flaky when mature and crumbly when aged.

Blue Cheshire
Blue Cheshire is veined with blue and green, hence its name. A rarer cheese than Cheshire, and a great favourite with epicures, the aged cheese has a rich flavour which is deliciously different.

Caerphilly
Caerphilly is a semi-soft cheese with a close, flaky texture, much like Cheddar, but white in colour. Caerphilly used to be made of partially skimmed milk but today it is manufactured from full-cream milk. There is still a very small farmhouse industry in Wales, where the cheese originated, but the majority of Caerphilly is produced by the Cheddar makers in the West Country of England. It is packed into small hoops while still warm to give a cheese weighing about 3.6 kg / 8 lb. Caerphilly is an unripened cheese, sold within days after it has been formed and soaked in brine.

● These very English cheeses are a fitting follow-up to game and, in particular, to a dish like grouse, which is quintessentially a bird of the British Isles. In this selection I have chosen two blue cheeses of differing character — one of them, Stilton, is one of the world's great blues. Cheddar is made world wide, but the perfect specimen, with the right degree of age and moistness, is still a cheese to be admired for its character as much as its usefulness; Caerphilly belongs to the same family but is light, young and supple in comparison. Allow 50 g /2 oz of each cheese per person.

  5 minutes

Veal

ITALIAN FAVOURITES

I nvite your friends round for a really elegant Italian meal. Start with a veal and tomato sauce served over the pasta of your choice; I think it is especially good with fresh fettucine.

For the main course serve delicate veal escalopes topped with a luxurious sauce and accompanied by tender asparagus. Paprika potatoes and Leek and curly endive salad make colourful side dishes, each adding a distinctive and refreshing flavour.

Finish in style with Pear delights, a crisp and creamy combination of ripe pears with a rich filling. Serve in individual dishes topped with smooth custard sprinkled with chopped nuts.

Fettucine alla capricciosa

*Sautéed veal escalopes
with asparagus*

Paprika potatoes

Leek and curly endive salad

Pear delights

Wine: Almaden Chenin Blanc

Fettucine alla capricciosa

Serves 4
125 g /4 oz stewing veal, finely diced
50 g /2 oz butter
salt and freshly ground black pepper
75 ml /5 tbls red wine
400 g /14 oz canned peeled tomatoes
30 ml /2 tbls tomato purée
50 g /2 oz mushrooms, finely sliced
1 slice Parma ham, or another raw ham, cut into strips
125 g /4 oz frozen peas, defrosted
225 g /8 oz fettucine
flat-leaved parsley, to garnish

1 Prepare the capricciosa sauce. In a small fryin-pan, heat half the butter. Add the finely diced veal and sauté over a high heat for 2 minutes, or until golden, turning with a spatula. Season to taste with salt and freshly ground black pepper. Pour in the red wine and simmer for 5 minutes, stirring occasionally with a wooden spoon.
2 In a saucepan, combine the canned tomatoes, with their juice, and the tomato purée with the veal and wine mixture and simmer gently for 20 minutes, stirring occasionally.
3 In a medium-sized frying-pan, heat the remaining butter. Add the prepared mushrooms and ham and sauté for 5 minutes, or until golden, tossing with a spatula.
4 Add the sautéed mushrooms and ham with the peas to the sauce mixture. Cook for 10 minutes, stirring occasionally. Adjust the seasoning and keep warm.
5 Meanwhile, bring a large saucepan of salted water to the boil. Add the fettucine and boil until *al dente* — cooked but still firm. Drain well and transfer to a heated serving dish. Pour the sauce over the fettucine and serve, garnished with a sprig of flat-leaved parsley.

● Fresh pasta will cook in a few minutes. Dried bought pasta will take longer, up to 12 minutes. Add a little olive oil to the water before you start cooking if using dried pasta.
● The sauce can be made ahead and reheated, if necessary.

 45 minutes

Plan-ahead timetable

On the morning of the meal
Pear delights: make the custard, cool it and transfer it to the refrigerator until required.

Three hours before the meal
Fettucine alla capricciosa: make the sauce.
Sautéed veal escalopes with asparagus: beat out the escalopes, season and leave to come to room temperature. Wash and trim the asparagus.
Paprika potatoes: peel and dice the potatoes.
Leek and curly endive salad: cook the leeks. Prepare the curly endive. Make the vinaigrette.

One hour before the meal
Sautéed veal escalopes with asparagus: cook the asparagus. Keep it warm.
Pear delights: prepare the pears and the filling. Chill until required.

Forty minutes before the meal
Paprika potatoes: cook, transfer to a serving dish and keep warm.

Fifteen minutes before the meal
Fettucine alla capricciosa: cook the pasta. Reheat the sauce, pour it over the pasta and serve.

Between the first and the main course
Sautéed veal escalopes with asparagus: cook the escalopes and keep them hot. Prepare the sauce, assemble and garnish.
Paprika potatoes: garnish. Serve.
Leek and curly endive salad: assemble the salad, spoon over a little vinaigrette and serve, with the remaining dressing passed separately.

Between the main course and the dessert
Pear delights: pour the custard over the pears, sprinkle with pistachio nuts and serve.

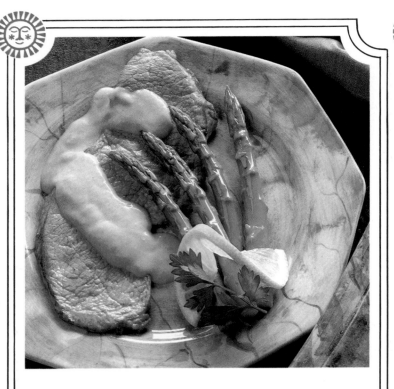

Sautéed veal escalopes with asparagus

Serves 4

4 × 75 g /3 oz veal escalopes
black pepper and salt
450 g /1 lb fresh asparagus
50 g /2 oz butter
1 egg yolk

45 ml /3 tbls thick cream
juice of 1 lemon
melted butter, to glaze
flat-leaved parsley and lemon
    twists, to garnish

1   Between 2 sheets of cling film, beat each escalope with a meat bat or rolling pin until very thin. Season generously with pepper. Allow to come to room temperature, then season with salt.
2   Meanwhile, prepare the asparagus. Wash the stalks thoroughly in cold water. Scrape the stems with a sharp knife to remove any scaly leaf points and cut off the tough, woody ends.
3   Bring a large saucepan of salted water to the boil. Add the prepared asparagus, bring back to the boil, then reduce the heat and simmer gently until cooked but not too soft. The thick part of the stem should feel tender when pierced with a knife. Drain the asparagus, reserving 90 ml /6 tbls cooking liquid. Keep warm.
4   Meanwhile, in a frying-pan large enough to take 2 of the escalopes comfortably in a single layer, heat half the butter. Sauté the escalopes for 30 seconds−1 minute each side, turning with a spatula. Carefully transfer to a heated serving dish or individual plates. Add the remaining butter to the pan and sauté the other escalopes. Transfer to the dish or plates and keep hot.
5   Remove the pan from the heat and allow to cool slightly.
6   In a small bowl, blend together the egg yolk, thick cream, lemon juice and reserved asparagus cooking liquid. Pour the mixture into the cooled pan and blend with a wooden spoon.
7   Cook over a low heat for 2 minutes, or until thickened, stirring constantly with the wooden spoon. (Do not allow the sauce to come to the boil, otherwise the egg will curdle.) Adjust the seasoning.
8   Arrange the asparagus on the dish or plates and garnish with flat-leaved parsley and lemon twists. Brush the asparagus with melted butter and spoon a little sauce over the meat. Serve the sauce separately in a heated sauce-boat.

bringing to room temperature, then 20−25 minutes

Almaden Chenin Blanc

Paprika potatoes

Serves 4

450 g /1 lb potatoes
30 ml /2 tbls olive oil
25 g /1 oz butter
1 small onion, finely chopped
5 ml /1 tsp paprika
salt and freshly ground black pepper
15 m /1 tbls finely snipped chives, to garnish

1   Peel and dice the potatoes. Pat them dry with absorbent paper.
2   In a medium-sized heavy-based saucepan, heat the olive oil and butter. When the foaming subsides, sauté the finely chopped onion for 5 minutes, or until slightly golden, stirring occasionally with a wooden spoon. Stir in the paprika and cook for a further minute.
3   Add the prepared potatoes to the onion and paprika mixture. Sauté over a high heat for 1−2 minutes, stirring constantly. Season to taste with salt and freshly ground black pepper.
4   Cover the pan, reduce the heat and cook the paprika potatoes over a low heat for 8−10 minutes, or until tender but not mushy, shaking the pan occasionally to prevent burning.
5   To serve, transfer the paprika potatoes to a heated serving dish. Garnish with finely snipped chives and serve as soon as possible.

30 minutes

Leek and curly endive salad

Serves 4

850 ml /1½ pt chicken stock, home-made or from a cube
8 young leeks
1 head curly endive
For the vinaigrette
90 ml /6 tbls olive oil
30 ml /2 tbls red wine vinegar
5 ml /1 tsp Dijon mustard
1 garlic clove, finely chopped
30 ml /2 tbls finely chopped fresh parsley
salt and freshly ground black pepper

1 In a large saucepan, bring the chicken stock to the boil.
2 Meanwhile, prepare the leeks. Cut off and discard the roots and the tough parts of the green leaves. Remove the outer leaves if necessary. Rinse the trimmed leeks thoroughly under cold running water to remove any dirt and grit.
3 Add the prepared leeks to the boiling stock, bring back to the boil, then reduce the heat, cover and cook for 20–25 minutes, or until tender but not too soft. Drain well and leave to get cold.
4 While the leeks are cooling, separate the curly endive leaves, discarding any discoloured, tough outer leaves and the stems. Wash well, drain and pat dry with a clean tea-towel.
5 Prepare the vinaigrette. In a bowl, combine the olive oil, red wine vinegar, Dijon mustard, finely chopped garlic and parsley. Season to taste with salt and freshly ground black pepper and beat with a fork until the mixture emulsifies.
6 In 4 individual serving dishes long enough to take the leeks, arrange a bed of curly endive leaves. Place 2 cold leeks side by side in the middle of each and spoon some of the vinaigrette over the leeks to coat them. Serve immediately, with the remaining vinaigrette in a sauce-boat.

 40 minutes and cooling

Pear delights

Serves 4

4 firm ripe pears
lemon juice, for brushing
200 ml /7 fl oz thick cream
30 ml /2 tbls caster sugar
15–30 ml /1–2 tbls kirsch
4×25 g /1 oz piece of trifle sponge
30 ml /2 tbls apricot jam, sieved
15 ml /1 tbls finely chopped
  pistachio nuts

For the custard
200 ml /7 fl oz milk
25 mm /1 in piece of vanilla pod,
  split, or 1.5 ml /¼ tsp vanilla
  essence
15–30 ml /1–2 tbls caster sugar
2.5 ml /½ tsp cornflour
3 egg yolks
butter, for greasing

1 First make the custard. If using a vanilla pod, place it and the milk in the top pan of a double boiler and scald over direct heat. Leave to infuse for 10–15 minutes. Mix the caster sugar and cornflour together in a large bowl, then whisk in the egg yolks until the mixture is pale and creamy and thick enough to leave a trail. Add the hot milk in a thin stream, whisking continuously.
2 Return to the top of a double boiler and place over simmering water for about 10 minutes, stirring continuously, until the custard is thick enough to coat the back of the spoon. Plunge into cold water to stop the cooking process, and continue to stir for 1–2 minutes while the custard cools slightly. Cool completely, then chill, covered with lightly buttered greaseproof paper until needed. If using vanilla essence, stir into the custard just before serving.
3 Keeping the pears whole and using an apple corer, core them from the bottom end. Remove and discard the stalks and pips.
4 Peel the pears. Hollow out the insides, leaving a 15 mm /½ in shell. Reserve the pulp and juice. Lightly brush the pears with lemon juice to prevent discoloration.
5 Chop the pulp and reserve for the filling.
6 Whisk the cream with the sugar to form soft peaks. Flavour with kirsch and stir in the reserved pear pulp and juice.
7 Carefully spoon the cream and pulp mixture into the pear shells.
8 Using a fluted biscuit cutter about 6.5 cm /2½ in in diameter, cut each piece of sponge into a round.
9 Spread each round with sieved apricot jam and place in an individual serving dish. Centre a pear shell on top. Pour the custard over the pears and sprinkle the top of each one with finely chopped pistachio nuts. Serve as soon as possible.

30 minutes making the custard, then 35 minutes

EASY ENTERTAINING

Artichoke salad

~

Veal in soured cream

Braised leeks with bacon

Noodles with caraway seeds

~

Honey and orange
ice cream

Wine: red bordeaux

Plan-ahead timetable

On the day before the meal
Honey and orange ice cream: make the ice cream and freeze it.

Two and a half hours before the meal
Honey and orange ice cream: prepare the julienne strips, blanch, drain and refresh.

Two hours before the meal
Artichoke salad: wash the lettuce and chill. Prepare the artichoke hearts, cook and chill. Cook the peas, prepare the tomatoes and watercress and chill.

One and a half hours before the meal
Veal in soured cream: sauté the veal and make the sauce; cook the onion and mushrooms; prepare the casserole and cook it.

One hour before the meal
Braised leeks with bacon: wash and prepare the leeks. Place in an ovenproof dish, add the butter and stock and transfer to the oven.
Artichoke salad: make the dressing.

I have a confession to make and I think it is one with which you will sympathize — sometimes I am willing to go all out when I am entertaining, but at other times I feel much lazier. This menu is especially for one of those lazy occasions. You can either make everything from scratch — still a simple menu to do — or cheat a bit with ready-prepared ingredients.

For a starter I have chosen Artichoke salad. If you make it with fresh artichoke hearts, it tastes wonderful, of course, but it is time-consuming to prepare — use canned artichoke hearts for speed. The hearts are filled with peas and studded with diced tomatoes and sprigs of watercress. This starter should be well chilled so it is best to chill all the ingredients before you assemble the salad. Serve it with a delicious, lemony mayonnaise.

The main course is nuggets of veal sautéed in butter and olive oil until lightly golden and then simmered in soured cream with buttered onions and mushrooms until it is fork tender. It sounds easy? It is, and what's more, this is a dish that can be popped into the oven and forgotten for an hour or so. Serve it garnished with thinly sliced lemon dipped in parsley and sprinkle more finely chopped parsley over the top of the veal.

With the creamy, pale-coloured veal I like to serve leeks braised whole in chicken stock and butter. They are tender and tasty and, for a finishing touch, I serve them topped with crumbled crispy bacon. Noodles with caraway seeds pair particularly well with Veal in soured cream. Ribbon noodles are cooked until just *al dente*, then drained and tossed in a mixture of caraway seeds and sautéed golden breadcrumbs.

To finish I suggest a creamy Honey and orange ice cream, home-made and garnished with julienne strips of orange. If you are feeling lazy, use a shop-bought vanilla or orange ice cream and add a spoonful or two of dark, liquid honey to each serving to disguise the fact that you haven't made it yourself.

Half an hour before the meal
Honey and orange ice cream: put the ice cream in the main part of the refrigerator to soften before serving.

Twenty minutes before the meal
Noodles with caraway seeds: cook the noodles, then keep warm in a colander set over a pan of simmering water.

Five minutes before the meal
Artichoke salad: assemble the salad; add the lemon juice to the mayonnaise and use to garnish the salad.

Between the first and the main course
Noodles with caraway seeds: quickly sauté the caraway seeds and breadcrumbs; add to the noodles and toss together gently.
Veal in soured cream: garnish and serve.
Braised leeks with bacon: grill the bacon until crisp, crumble over the leeks and serve.

Between the main course and the dessert
Honey and orange ice cream: transfer the ice cream to one large or six individual serving dishes, sprinkle on the orange julienne and serve.

Artichoke salad

Serves 6
6 large globe artichokes
1 lettuce
juice of 1½ lemons
salt
75 g /3 oz frozen green peas, cooked and chilled
1–2 large firm tomatoes, blanched, skinned, seeded, diced and chilled
6 sprigs watercress, chilled

For the dressing
15 ml /1 tbls wine vinegar or lemon juice
salt
freshly ground black pepper
a pinch of dry or French mustard
45 ml /3 tbls olive oil
For the lemon mayonnaise
225 ml /8 fl oz mayonnaise
15 ml /1 tbls lemon juice

1 Wash and dry the lettuce. Shred it finely, wrap it in a tea-towel and chill.
2 To prepare the artichoke hearts, first prepare a bowl of acidulated water by adding the juice of half a lemon to about 1.5 L /3 pt water. Break off the stalks from the artichokes, strip off all the outer leaves, then slice around the heart to remove those leaves closest to it. Cut away any remaining stalk, leaving the hairy choke in place. To prevent them discolouring, drop the artichoke hearts into the bowl of acidulated water until ready to use.
3 To cook, reserve 15 ml /1 tbls lemon juice, add the remaining lemon juice to a pan of salted water, bring to simmering point, add the hearts and cook until tender (15–20 minutes). Lift out with a slotted spoon, drain thoroughly on absorbent paper and carefully remove the hairy choke with a small sharp knife and a teaspoon. Sprinkle with the reserved lemon juice and chill.
4 To make the dressing, in a bowl mix the vinegar or lemon juice with a generous pinch of salt and freshly ground black pepper to taste. Add the mustard. Beat in the olive oil with a fork until the dressing emulsifies.
5 When ready to serve, toss the chilled lettuce with the dressing and arrange on individual plates. Place an artichoke heart on each bed of lettuce. Spoon the chilled cooked peas onto the hearts, followed by the chilled diced tomato, and garnish with tiny sprigs of chilled watercress. Combine the mayonnaise with the lemon juice and spoon 30 ml /2 tbls of lemon mayonnaise onto the lettuce at one side of the artichoke heart.

● This dish is made more quickly with canned artichoke hearts. If these are small, you may have to serve 2 to each person.

 40 minutes, plus chilling

Veal in soured cream

Serves 6
1.1 kg /2½ lb boned shoulder or leg of veal
salt and freshly ground black pepper
50 g /2 oz butter
30 ml /2 tbls olive oil
15 ml /1 tbls flour
275 ml /10 fl oz soured cream
2.5 ml /½ tsp paprika
60–90 ml /4–6 tbls finely chopped onion
225 g /8 oz button mushrooms, quartered
30 ml /2 tbls lemon juice
For the garnish
1 lemon, halved lengthways and cut into slices
30 ml /2 tbls finely chopped fresh parsley

1 Heat the oven to 170C /325F /gas 3. Cut the veal into 4 cm /1½ in
cubes. Season generously with salt and freshly ground black pepper,
rubbing the seasoning well into the meat.
2 Heat 25 g /1 oz of the butter with the olive oil in a thick-bottomed
frying-pan and sauté the meat, a few pieces at a time, until it is lightly
browned on all sides. Remove it with a slotted spoon and place it in a
flameproof casserole.
3 Add the flour to the fat left in the frying-pan and cook, stirring
constantly, for 2–3 minutes until smooth. Add the soured cream and
cook, stirring, until well blended. Season with salt, freshly ground
black pepper and paprika. Pour this over the meat in the casserole.
4 Melt the remaining butter and sauté the finely chopped onion until
golden. Add the quartered mushrooms and the lemon juice and simmer
over a low heat for 5 minutes. Pour these over the veal and soured
cream mixture and mix well. Cover the casserole and cook in the oven
for 1 hour, or until the veal is tender. Transfer to a heated dish and
serve immediately garnished with lemon slices dipped in parsley and
the remaining parsley sprinkled over the veal.

1½ hours   red bordeaux

Braised leeks
with bacon

Serves 6
12 large or 18 small leeks
75–125 g /3–4 oz butter
500 ml /18 fl oz chicken stock, home-made or from a cube
freshly ground black pepper
225 g /8 oz thinly sliced bacon

1 Heat the oven to 170C /325F /gas 3. Trim the leeks, then split
each one lengthways through to the middle and down to within
7.5 cm /3 in of the base. Wash the leeks thoroughly in cold water and
drain well.
2 Select a shallow ovenproof dish large enough to hold the leeks in a
single layer. Use some of the butter to grease the dish generously.
Arrange the leeks over the base of the dish and dot with the remaining
butter. Pour the chicken stock over the leeks and season to taste with
freshly ground black pepper.
3 Braise the leeks, uncovered, in the oven for 45–50 minutes, or until
tender.
4 Meanwhile, grill the bacon until crisp and crumble it into small
pieces. Scatter the crumbled bacon over the braised leeks and serve
immediately.

● Leeks are tiresome things to wash as grit can get embedded between
the layers. To clean them thoroughly, split them as described and wash
them. Then stand the leeks upside down in a pan of cold water for 2
minutes; the dirt will sink in the water.

1 hour

Noodles with caraway seeds

Serves 6
350 g /12 oz ribbon noodles
salt
50 g /2 oz butter
45 ml /3 tbls caraway seeds
120 ml /8 tbls fresh white breadcrumbs
freshly ground black pepper

1 Bring a saucepan of salted water to the boil and add the noodles. Simmer gently for 12–15 minutes until *al dente* — cooked through, but still firm.
2 Meanwhile, melt the butter in a frying-pan, add the caraway seeds and breadcrumbs and sauté for 4–5 minutes until the breadcrumbs are golden, stirring constantly.
3 Drain the noodles thoroughly and place them in a heated serving dish. Sprinkle the breadcrumbs and caraway seeds over the noodles, season to taste with freshly ground black pepper and toss gently. Serve immediately.

● The noodles can be prepared a little in advance: keep them warm in a colander set over a pan of simmering water. Toss with the breadcrumbs and caraway seeds just before serving.

 25 minutes

Honey and orange ice cream

Serves 6
275 g /10 oz sugar
600 ml /1 pt milk
275 ml /10 fl oz thick cream
5 ml /1 tsp grated orange zest

8 medium-sized egg yolks
60 ml /4 tbls clear honey
15 ml /1 tbls orange juice
To garnish
1 large orange

1 If you are using the freezing compartment of a refrigerator, turn it to the coldest setting one hour before making the ice cream.
2 To make a rich custard, combine the sugar, milk, thick cream and orange zest in a pan and bring to the boil. Remove the pan from the heat; cover and leave to infuse for 5–10 minutes.
3 In the top pan of a double boiler beat the egg yolks lightly. Pour in the infused orange cream, stirring, until the custard mixture is light and foamy. Stand the pan on a boiler containing simmering water and cook over a low heat, stirring constantly with a wooden spoon until the custard thickens enough to coat the back of a spoon.
4 Pour the custard into a bowl and cover with a plate. Set the bowl in a larger bowl filled with iced water and let the custard cool completely.
5 Stir the honey and orange juice into the cooled custard. Chill the custard, covered, for 2 hours.
6 Pour the custard into a metal loaf tin or freezer-proof container. Cover and freeze until the mixture begins to harden 25 mm /1 in around the sides of the container, about 1–2 hours.
7 Remove the ice cream from the freezer and beat it with a whisk or fork. Return to the freezer until it is firmly frozen: 3–4 hours.
8 About 30 minutes before serving, transfer the ice cream to the main part of the refrigerator to soften.
9 Meanwhile, to prepare a garnish of julienne strips, pare away the zest of the orange with a potato peeler — there should not be any pith attached. Cut the zest into very fine shreds about the length of a matchstick, 4 cm /1½ in long and 3 mm /⅛ in wide.
10 Place the julienne strips in a small pan, cover with water, bring to the boil and simmer for 5–6 minutes, drain and refresh under cold running water.
11 To serve, scoop the slightly softened ice cream into a glass dish or individual serving dishes and sprinkle with the orange julienne.

20 minutes plus chilling,
then 4–6 hours freezing

Prawn skewers

Stuffed veal birds

Sautéed parsnips

Broad beans and lettuce

Tarte aux figues

*Blackcurrant and
caramel cream*

Wine: red Graves

Plan-ahead timetable

On the day before the meal
Tarte aux figues (if using): make and half bake the pastry case.

On the morning of the meal
Tarte aux figues (if using): prepare and chill.
Blackcurrant and caramel cream (if using): prepare the blackcurrant cream and chill. Make the caramel.

One and a quarter hours before the meal
Prawn skewers: prepare the prawns and marinate.
Stuffed veal birds: make the stuffing, stuff and tie up.

One hour before the meal
Stuffed veal birds: sauté the onions, veal birds and carrots. Add the stock and braise.
Broad beans and lettuce: prepare the vegetables.
Tarte aux figues (if using): decorate with whipped cream.
Blackcurrant and caramel cream (if using): add the caramel.

Thirty minutes before the meal
Broad beans and lettuce: sauté onions, add beans and simmer.
Sautéed parsnips: prepare, blanch, drain and dry.

Fifteen minutes before the meal
Prawn skewers: heat the grill. Thread the skewers.
Sautéed parsnips: sauté and keep warm.
Broad beans and lettuce: add the lettuce, seasoning and stock. Simmer, transfer to a serving dish and keep warm.

Just before the meal
Prawn skewers: grill, garnish with lemon twists and serve.

Between the first and the main course
Stuffed veal birds: transfer to serving dish, garnish and serve.

Prawn skewers

Serves 4
20 large boiled prawns in their shells, about 225 g /8 oz
20 green olives, stoned
olive oil, for greasing
4 thin lemon slices, to garnish
For the Chinese oyster and soy marinade
15 ml /1 tbls oyster sauce
15 ml /1 tbls soy sauce
15 ml /1 tbls honey
30 ml /2 tbls dry white wine
30 ml /2 tbls peanut oil
a pinch of cayenne pepper
a dash of chilli sauce or Tabasco

1 Prepare the marinade. In a small bowl, combine the oyster sauce, soy sauce, honey, dry white wine and peanut oil. Season to taste with cayenne pepper and chilli sauce or Tabasco. Mix the ingredients until they are well blended.
2 Peel the legs and saddle shell from the body of each prawn, leaving the head and the tail shells in place.
3 Add the prawns to the marinade and stir until each prawn is well coated. Leave them to marinate for about 1 hour.
4 Heat the grill to high.
5 Select four 15 cm /6 in skewers. Thread a skewer through the tail of a prawn, then sideways through an olive, then through the head of the same prawn. Repeat, using 5 prawns and 5 olives on each skewer. Brush them well with the marinade.
6 Brush the grill grid with the olive oil. Place the skewers side by side on the grid. Grill them 7.5 cm /3 in from the heat for 1½ minutes on each side, or until they are heated through, brushing the skewers with marinade when you turn them.
7 Arrange the skewers on a heated serving dish. To garnish, cut each lemon slice to the centre and make a twist to fit over one end of each of the skewers. Serve them immediately.

10 minutes, marinating for 1 hour, then 20 minutes

Stuffed veal birds

Serves 4
12 × 50 g /2 oz thin escalopes of veal
salt and ground black pepper
75 g /3 oz butter
15 ml /1 tbls olive oil
1 Spanish onion, finely chopped
24 baby carrots
425 ml /15 fl oz well-flavoured chicken stock, home-made or from a cube
1 bay leaf
5 cm /2 in piece of celery stick
3–4 sprigs of parsley
sprigs of parsley, to garnish

For the forcemeat stuffing
50 g /2 oz fresh white breadcrumbs
50 g /2 oz freshly grated suet
100 g /4 oz cooked ham, chopped
45 ml /3 tbls freshly chopped parsley
1.5 ml /¼ tsp dried thyme
1.5 ml /¼ tsp dried marjoram
5 ml /1 tsp grated lemon zest
2 eggs, lightly beaten
juice of ½ lemon
salt
freshly ground black pepper

1 Prepare the forcemeat stuffing. In a bowl, mix the breadcrumbs, grated suet, chopped ham and parsley, dried thyme and marjoram, lemon zest, lightly beaten eggs and lemon juice. Season to taste.
2 Place the veal escalopes between 2 sheets of cling film or wet greaseproof paper and beat them with a rolling pin or meat bat to flatten and tenderize them. Season generously with salt and freshly ground black pepper. Divide the forcemeat mixture among the escalopes, spreading it out but leaving the edges free. Roll up the escalopes and tie at each end with very fine string.
3 In a heavy-based saucepan or flameproof casserole, heat 25 g /1 oz of the butter and the olive oil. When the foaming subsides, gently sauté the onion for 10 minutes, or until transparent, stirring with a wooden spoon. Remove the onion with a slotted spoon and reserve.
4 Add 25 g /1 oz butter to the pan and cook the veal birds over a moderate heat until well browned.
5 In another pan, heat the remaining butter and cook the baby carrots over a moderate heat for 5 minutes, or until they are lightly browned all over, shaking the pan occasionally.
6 Add the browned carrots and the sautéed onion to the veal birds. Pour in the stock and add the bay leaf, celery and parsley. Cover and simmer gently for 40 minutes, or until tender.
7 To serve, transfer the veal birds to a heated dish. Snip and remove the strings. With a slotted spoon, arrange the baby carrots around the veal birds. Season the pan juices to taste and strain them over the veal birds. Garnish and serve.

1¼ hours   red Graves

Sautéed parsnips

Serves 4
550−700 g /1¼−1½ lb parsnips
salt
40 g /1½ oz butter
15 ml /1 tbls olive oil
freshly ground black pepper
freshly snipped chives, to garnish

1 Peel the parsnips and cut off the tops. If the root has a woody tip, or the centre of the root seems excessively woody, then trim this away. Slice each parsnip into 3 mm /⅛ in thick rounds.
2 Bring a saucepan of salted water to the boil, add the parsnips and blanch for 3 minutes. Drain, rinse them under cold running water and then drain them again. Pat the parsnips completely dry with absorbent paper.
3 In a large frying-pan, heat the butter and olive oil. When the foaming subsides, sauté the blanched parsnips over a moderate heat for 10 minutes, or until they are tender and golden brown, tossing the slices frequently with a spatula. Season to taste with salt and freshly ground black pepper.
4 Transfer the parsnips to a heated gratin dish. Garnish them with the snipped chives and serve immediately.

25 minutes

Broad beans and lettuce

Serves 4
350 g /12 oz shelled broad beans, fresh or frozen
8 button onions
½ small lettuce
25 g /1 oz butter
15 ml /1 tbls olive oil
1.5 ml /¼ tsp crumbled dried savory or dried thyme
a pinch of caster sugar
salt and freshly ground black pepper
30 ml /2 tbls beef stock, made with a cube
1.5 ml /¼ tsp Worcestershire sauce
1.5 ml /¼ tsp soy sauce
30 ml /2 tbls finely chopped, fresh parsley

1 If using fresh beans, remove the grey outer skins of any beans that seem large and tough. Slit the skin along the indented edge with your thumbnail, then squeeze out the pale green kernel.
2 Peel the button onions carefully.
3 Separate the lettuce leaves, wash them in cold water and drain them thoroughly.
4 In a medium-sized saucepan, heat the butter and olive oil. When the foaming subsides, sauté the button onions over a moderate heat for 10 minutes, or until they are golden brown, shaking the pan constantly.
5 Add the broad beans, cover and cook gently for 5 minutes if using frozen beans, 10−12 minutes if using fresh beans.
6 When the beans are tender but still firm, add the drained lettuce, savory or thyme and sugar. Season to taste with salt and freshly ground black pepper. Moisten with beef stock, add the Worcestershire and soy sauces and simmer gently for a further 5 minutes, stirring occasionally with a wooden spoon.
7 Turn the broad beans, the button onions and the lettuce with their cooking juices into a deep, heated serving dish. Sprinkle them with finely chopped parsley and serve immediately.

30−40 minutes

Tarte aux figues

Serves 4–6
21–23 cm /8½–9 in half-baked
  shortcrust pastry case
1 medium-sized egg white,
  beaten
For the crème pâtissière
100 g /4 oz caster sugar
30 ml /2 tbls cornflour
575 ml /1 pt milk

4 egg yolks
50 g /2 oz butter, diced
1.5–2.5 ml /¼–½ tsp vanilla
  essence
For the topping
350 g /12 oz canned figs
30 ml /2 tbls icing sugar
15 ml /1 tbls kirsch
150 ml /5 fl oz thick cream

1 Place the half-baked pastry case on a baking sheet. Brush the inside with beaten egg white.
2 Prepare the crème pâtissière filling. Combine the sugar and cornflour in a saucepan. Add the milk, stirring and making sure there are no lumps. Slowly bring to the boil over a medium heat, stirring constantly. Simmer for 3–4 minutes, stirring until the mixture thickens and no longer tastes floury. Remove from the heat.
3 In a large bowl, beat the egg yolks until blended. Add the hot sauce to the beaten yolks in a thin stream, beating vigorously.
4 Strain the custard through a fine sieve into a large bowl. Beat in the diced butter, piece by piece, until it is completely melted and incorporated into the custard. Leave to cool until it is lukewarm.
5 Heat the oven to 170C /325F /gas 3.
6 Flavour the cooled custard with vanilla essence. Pour the filling into the pastry case, then bake for 30 minutes, or until the custard is set. Remove the tart from the oven and leave to cool.
7 Make the topping. Drain the figs and reserve the syrup. Cut the figs in half lengthways and drain them well on absorbent paper. Arrange the halved figs over the tart, leaving a narrow border around the outer edge.
8 In a small saucepan combine 50 ml /2 fl oz of the reserved fig syrup with the icing sugar, beating vigorously until the sugar has dissolved. Place the pan over a medium heat and boil until the syrup has reduced to half its original quantity.
9 Remove it from the heat. Stir the kirsch into the syrup. Spoon the kirsch-flavoured syrup over the figs. Cool, then chill the tart.
10 Before serving, whip the cream until thick. Spoon it into a piping bag and pipe it around the outer edge of the tart.

 making and baking the pastry case,
then 1 hour, plus cooling and chilling

Blackcurrant and caramel cream

Serves 4
250 g /8 oz blackcurrants
150 g /5 oz sugar
150 ml /5 fl oz thick cream, whipped
2.5–5 ml /½–1 tsp ground cinnamon
oil, for greasing

1 Rinse the blackcurrants, then remove the stalks. Place them in a heavy-based saucepan with 25 g /1 oz of the sugar. Put the pan over a low heat and heat gently for 5–10 minutes until the blackcurrants are cooked, then leave them until they are cold.
2 Spoon the blackcurrants into 4 bowls or tall-stemmed glasses. Mix the whipped cream and cinnamon together and spoon the mixture over the blackcurrants, then chill.
3 To make the caramel topping, place the remaining sugar in a small pan. Put over a medium heat for about 5 minutes until the sugar turns into a golden liquid. Avoid stirring — just tilt the pan constantly from side to side.
4 Cover a baking tray with foil and oil it very well. Quickly pour the caramel in a thin layer onto the foil and set it aside until the caramel is set firm. Roll the edges of the foil over the caramel and break it up by thumping it hard with a hammer or rolling pin. The broken caramel should look like splintered glass. Sprinkle the chips over the cream and chill.

● The caramel can be made a few hours ahead, provided it is kept in a dry place. It can be put on the cream approximately 1 hour before serving. Humidity will make the caramel sticky and eventually melt it if it is made too far in advance.

 15 minutes plus chilling,
then 30 minutes for making the caramel

Pork

COUNTRY-STYLE ENTERTAINING

Haricot bean soup

*Braised pork
with apple rings*

*Herbed green beans
with garlic*

*Tossed green salad
with Cheddar dressing*

English walnut tart

Wine: Vacqueyras

Plan-ahead timetable

On the day before the meal
Haricot bean soup: soak the beans.

On the morning of the meal
English walnut tart: make the pastry and the filling. Fill the tart and bake.

Two and three quarter hours before the meal
Haricot bean soup: drain the beans and start to cook.
Braised pork with apple rings: prepare both joint and stuffing and stuff the meat.

One and a half hours before the meal
Braised pork with apple rings: prepare roasting tin; cook pork.
Tossed green salad with Cheddar dressing: wash the lettuce, endive and chicory and chill. Prepare the dressing.

Forty-five minutes before the meal
Haricot bean soup: purée half the beans and combine with the remaining beans and stock.

The true art of entertaining comes from knowing and being yourself and living by your own standards, not those of others. You can find fascinating ways — well within your means — to entertain anyone, from a visiting diplomat to a member of the family, without trying to do what is 'expected'.

Of course, feather-light quenelles, glittering aspics and ethereal soufflés are part and parcel of good cooking and I enjoy these. But give me a really simple meal with texture and flavour — the kind that one can eat with sleeves rolled up at a country table anywhere in the world — and you will see my eyes light up with genuine pleasure. This menu, for a casual dinner for six, is a case in point.

The first course is Haricot bean soup, a lovely country-style soup that I first tasted in Rome; it's an intriguing combination of dried white beans, both whole and puréed, with chicken stock, enlivened just before serving with a sprinkling of pure olive oil and a hint of finely chopped garlic and parsley. It is a rustic soup with a great deal of flavour.

For the main course there is a chined loin of pork. Each handsome chop is cut almost to the bone to hold a succulent breadcrumb, onion, apple and herb filling; the joint is then braised in a mixture of cider and stock to give it a full and hearty flavour. Served with crisp fried apple rings, the dish is a cleverly designed combination of colour, tang and texture. With the pork I like to serve tender young green beans, parboiled so they are still crisp to the bite, then tossed in a herb and garlic butter. Also offer your guests a refreshing green salad of lettuce, curly endive and chicory complemented by a flavoursome Cheddar dressing and you have a main course that will be memorable despite its simplicity.

To complete this meal there is an English walnut tart which is crunchy and nutty with a rich treacle filling. It's at its very best when served with an orange-flavoured whipped cream and small cups of piping hot black coffee.

English walnut tart: decorate it with whipped cream and then refrigerate until needed.
Herbed green beans with garlic: prepare, cook, refresh and drain the beans.
Braised pork with apple rings: remove the foil and continue to cook the pork.

Fifteen minutes before the meal
Braised pork with apple rings: core and slice the apples, fry and keep warm.

Five minutes before the meal
Haricot bean soup: reheat the soup, cook the garlic; combine the ingredients and garnish.

Between the first and the main course
Tossed green salad with Cheddar dressing: add the dressing and toss, then add the grated cheese and toss again.
Braised pork with apple rings: garnish and serve with the skimmed pan juices.
Herbed green beans with garlic: combine the herbs and the butter, heat the beans and serve.

Haricot bean soup

Serves 6
350 g /12 oz white haricot beans
1 Spanish onion, finely chopped
2½ chicken stock cubes
1 bay leaf
salt and freshly ground black pepper
a pinch of cayenne pepper
60 ml /4 tbls olive oil
2 garlic cloves, finely chopped
30 ml /2 tbls finely chopped fresh parlsey

1   Soak the beans overnight in cold water. Drain them and put them into a pan with 2 L /3½ pt cold water, the onion, chicken stock cubes and bay leaf. Do not add salt as this toughens the beans. Bring to the boil, cover and simmer the beans as slowly as possible for 1½–2 hours, or until they are tender.
2   Discard the bay leaf and strain the beans through a sieve, reserving the stock, then put half the beans back into the pan; purée the remaining beans in a blender and add these puréed beans to the whole beans. Add 420–600 ml /15 fl oz–1 pt of the reserved cooking stock or enough to make the soup up to 1.1 L /2 pt. A little more stock can be added if necessary, but be careful not to overdo it or the soup will separate. Season to taste with salt, freshly ground black pepper and cayenne pepper.
3   Reheat the soup. Heat the olive oil in a small saucepan and sauté the chopped garlic in it until it is just golden. Add the chopped parsley to this mixture and pour it into the soup. Serve very hot.

● A word of warning — it is very important to obtain white kidney-shaped haricot beans. The wrong type of bean does not soften when cooked and produces a bitter-tasting stock.

soaking the beans overnight, then 2½ hours

Braised pork with apple rings

Serves 6

2–2.3 kg /4½–5 lb loin of pork, chined
75 ml /5 tbls olive oil
75 g /3 oz butter
1½ Spanish onions, finely chopped
450 g /1 lb white breadcrumbs
25 g /1 oz chopped suet
15–30 ml /1–2 tbls chopped fresh thyme
90 ml /6 tbls chopped parsley

450 g /1 lb cooking apples, finely chopped
salt and ground black pepper
1 egg
15–30 ml /1–2 tbls lemon juice
15–30 ml /1–2 tbls milk, if needed
150 ml /5 fl oz cider
425 ml /15 fl oz chicken stock, home-made or from a cube
3 red dessert apples
6–8 parsley sprigs

1 Heat the oven to 190C /375F /gas 5. To prepare the meat, trim the fat down to an even thickness of 20 mm /¾ in. Heat 60 ml /4 tbls olive oil in a frying-pan and brown the joint on all sides.
2 To make the stuffing, melt 50 g /2 oz butter in the pan and sauté the onion gently until soft. Remove the onion and combine in a large bowl with the breadcrumbs, suet, thyme, 60 ml /4 tbls parsley and the chopped cooking apples. Season with salt and freshly ground black pepper to taste. Add the egg and lemon juice and mix the stuffing to a paste. If the mixture is too dry, add a little milk.
3 To stuff the joint, separate the loin of pork as if into chops by cutting down almost to the bone. Fill the space between each chop generously with stuffing — the stuffing band should be as wide as the chop. Use long skewers horizontally to keep the chops together. Season the top of the joint with salt and freshly ground black pepper and sprinkle the stuffing bands with the remaining chopped parsley.
4 Pour the cider and the stock into a roasting tin and bring to the boil on top of the cooker. Place the joint in the tin, cover with foil and cook in the oven for 45 minutes. Remove the foil and cook the joint for a further 45 minutes–1 hour.
5 When the pork is almost done, core but do not peel the eating apples, slice them into rings and fry them in the remaining butter and olive oil until golden.
6 To serve, transfer the braised pork to a warmed serving dish, remove the skewers and garnish with the fried apples and the parsley sprigs. Skim the fat from the pan juices and serve the juices in a heated sauce-boat.

 2 hours

Vacqueyras or another Côtes-du-Rhône red

Herbed green beans with garlic

Serves 6

700 g /1½ lb baby green beans
salt
50 g /2 oz butter
30 ml /2 tbls finely chopped fresh chervil
30 ml /2 tbls finely chopped fresh parsley
30 ml /2 tbls finely snipped fresh chives
1–2 garlic cloves, finely chopped
freshly ground black pepper
extra chervil, parsley and chives to garnish (optional)

1 Top and tail the green beans — they should be young enough not to require stringing.
2 Bring a pan of salted water to the boil. Add the beans, bring the water back to simmering point and cook gently for 2–5 minutes, or until the beans are just tender but still slightly crisp to the bite.
3 Drain the beans and plunge them into cold water for 2–5 minutes to stop the cooking process and refresh them. Leave them to drain.
4 Combine the butter with the finely chopped herbs and garlic, and season with a little salt and freshly ground black pepper.
5 When ready to serve, place the herb butter in a pan and melt it gently. Add the beans and toss, adding a generous seasoning of salt and freshly ground black pepper. Cover and cook until the beans are heated through. Serve at once with the buttery juices poured over, and garnish with fresh herbs if you wish.

25 minutes

Tossed green salad with Cheddar dressing

Serves 6
1 small round lettuce
1 small head curly endive
1 head white chicory
60 ml /4 tbls finely chopped parsley
30 ml /2 tbls finely chopped chives or spring onion tops
2.5 ml /½ tsp mustard powder
15 ml /1 tbls wine vinegar
120 ml /8 tbls olive oil
1 small garlic clove, finely chopped
30 ml /2 tbls lemon juice
salt and freshly ground black pepper
50 g /2 oz Cheddar cheese, finely grated

1   Wash the lettuce, endive and white chicory, separating out the leaves and discarding any bruised or discoloured ones. Dry the leaves individually, wrap them in a clean cloth and leave them to crisp up in the vegetable compartment of the refrigerator.
2   Break the salad greens into a salad bowl in fairly large pieces. Sprinkle with the finely chopped parsley and chives or spring onion tops and toss well.
3   Blend the mustard powder with the wine vinegar until smooth. Add the olive oil, together with the finely chopped garlic and lemon juice, and beat with a fork until the ingredients form an emulsion. Season with salt and freshly ground black pepper to taste.
4   Pour the dressing over the salad and toss thoroughly. Sprinkle the salad with the finely grated Cheddar cheese, toss again and serve immediately.

🔪 20–25 minutes

English walnut tart

Serves 6
225 g /8 oz flour
5 ml /1 tsp icing sugar
2.5 ml /½ tsp salt
150 g /5 oz cold butter, diced
1 medium-sized egg yolk
5 ml /1 tsp lemon juice
30 ml /2 tbls iced water
For the filling
50 g /2 oz unsalted butter
100 g /4 oz sugar

3 eggs
75 ml /3 fl oz molasses
75 ml /3 fl oz golden syrup
juice of ½ lemon
100 g /4 oz broken walnuts
1 egg white
12 walnut halves
15–30 ml /1–2 tbls grated orange zest
275 ml /10 fl oz thick cream, whipped and chilled

1   Sift the flour, icing sugar and salt into a bowl. Add the butter and cut in until the mixture resembles fine breadcrumbs. Beat the egg yolk with the lemon juice and 15 ml /1 tbls of the water. Add this to the flour mixture and mix well. Stir in the remaining water and shape the pastry into a ball. Chill for 1 hour.
2   Heat the oven to 230C /450F /gas 8.
3   Roll the pastry out to a depth of 5 mm /¼ in and use to line a 23 cm /9 in flan tin. Prick the base well.
4   Cream the butter and sugar with an electric whisk, add the whole eggs, molasses, golden syrup and lemon juice and whisk in well. Fold in the broken walnuts.
5   Whisk the egg white until it forms stiff peaks and, with a metal spoon, fold it gently into the filling mixture. Pour the mixture into the pastry-lined tin. Arrange the walnut halves decoratively on the surface of the tart.
6   Bake in the oven for 10 minutes, then reduce the heat to 180C /350F /gas 4 and continue to bake for a further 25 minutes. Remove the tart from the oven and leave it to cool.
7   Fold the grated orange zest into the chilled whipped cream and pipe between the walnut halves on the cold tart.

🔪🔪 making the pastry case, chilling, then 1 hour

PORK FOR A SPECIAL OCCASION

Little Mozzarella cigars is an appetizer based on the great Italian favourite, *Mozzarella in carozza*. The original consists of slices of Mozzarella cheese sandwiched between two slices of bread, dipped in beaten egg and milk, then deep fried until crisp. My rolled version has less bread, and therefore more fresh creamy cheese, and I spread my bread with a little Dijon mustard for additional flavour. I also find pan frying quite sufficient to cook the cigars crisply, and many people consider it easier and less worrying than deep frying. Arrange the fried cigars in a golden pile and garnish them with tomato wedges, watercress sprigs and black olives.

For those many people who like a traditional roast, the main course will be a treat — with a difference. I've decided to follow my little cheese tasties with a delicious winter dish of Roast pork with dried fruits. Score the skin of a lean loin of pork and roast it surrounded by a sweet-savoury mixture of plump prunes, apricots, apple and thyme.

Serve it with Individual rice moulds. This simple accompaniment is quick and easy to prepare, yet the little rice turrets — attractively speckled with sweetcorn — will add that special touch. To complete the course serve Steamed peas with ham fingers. Steam the peas lightly with chopped spring onions, flavour them with lemon juice and combine them with juicy sautéed strips of ham.

Californian wines are fast becoming more available. Why not try the delicious Beaulieu Pinot Chardonnay from the Napa Valley, near San Francisco. It will go well with your roast pork, as will most whites made from the reliable Californian Chardonnay grape.

To finish the meal, try my way of making Rhubarb compote with redcurrant jelly. Cut into neat batons, then sweetened with a good helping of redcurrant jelly, the rhubarb is cooked in the oven. It holds its shape well and has a light and delicate flavour. I like it cold, accompanied by thick cream, but it is also excellent hot.

Mozzarella cigars

*Roast loin of pork
with dried fruits*

*Individual rice moulds
with sweetcorn*

Steamed peas with ham fingers

*Rhubarb compote
with redcurrant jelly*

Wine: Beaulieu Pinot Chardonnay.

Mozzarella cigars

Serves 4
8 slices of sliced white bread
20–25 ml /4–5 tsp Dijon mustard
225 g /8 oz Mozzarella cheese
freshly ground black pepper
100 g /4 oz butter
To garnish
4 tomato wedges
2 black olives, halved
sprigs of watercress

1 Cut the crusts off the bread and roll each slice until very thin, using a rolling pin.
2 Spread each slice with a little Dijon mustard to taste.
3 Slice the Mozzarella as thinly as possible and cover each slice of bread with pieces of cheese. Season generously with freshly ground black pepper.
4 Roll up each Mozzarella-covered slice of bread very tightly and secure with a wooden cocktail stick, making a 'stitch' through the loose edge along the length of the roll.
5 Select a frying-pan large enough to take the Mozzarella cigars in a single layer. Heat the butter, then lay the cigars side by side in the pan and sauté them for 2 minutes, or until they are evenly browned and the cheese has melted inside. Turn them once with a spatula and shake the pan frequently.
6 Remove the cigars from the pan with the spatula and drain them well on absorbent paper to absorb the excess fat. Remove the cocktail sticks from the cigars.
7 Arrange the Mozzarella cigars on a heated serving dish. Garnish them with the tomato wedges, halved black olives and sprigs of watercress. Serve the cigars immediately.

Plan-ahead timetable

On the day before the meal
Roast loin of pork with dried fruits: soak the dried fruits.

Four hours before the meal
Roast loin of pork with dried fruits: bring the pork to room temperature.
Steamed peas with ham fingers: defrost the peas.
Individual rice moulds with sweetcorn: defrost the sweetcorn.
Rhubarb compote with redcurrant jelly: cook.

One and a half hours before the meal
Mozzarella cigars: prepare the cigars.
Roast loin of pork with dried fruits: roast. Drain the fruits and mix with the onion and the seasoning.

One hour before the meal
Roast loin of pork with dried fruits: add the fruit mixture.
Return to the oven and lower temperature. Prepare apples.

Forty-five minutes before the meal
Roast loin of pork with dried fruits: add the apples.
Steamed peas with ham fingers: prepare the ingredients.
Individual rice moulds with sweetcorn: cook the rice. Mix it with the sweetcorn and spoon the mixture into the ramekins. Place them on a baking tray and cover them with foil.

Ten minutes before the meal
Mozzarella cigars: cook and serve.
Steamed peas with ham fingers: cook and keep warm.
Individual rice moulds with sweetcorn: bake.

Between the first and the main course
Roast loin of pork with dried fruits: transfer it to a serving dish, add the sauce and serve.
Steamed peas with ham fingers: combine the ingredients. Serve.
Individual rice moulds with sweetcorn: turn out and serve.

 30 minutes

Roast loin of pork with dried fruits

Serves 4

900 g /2 lb lean loin of pork, chined but with the skin left on
15 ml /1 tbls olive oil
salt and freshly ground black pepper
100 g /4 oz prunes, soaked overnight
100 g /4 oz dried apricots, soaked overnight
2 Spanish onions, very coarsely chopped
a generous pinch of dried thyme
15 g /½ oz butter
2 tart, crisp eating apples
lemon juice

1 Remove the pork from the refrigerator about 2 hours before you intend to roast it. Leave it to come to room temperature.
2 Heat the oven to 230C /450F /gas 8.
3 Wipe the pork with a damp cloth. If there are any bristles on the skin, singe them off over an open flame.
4 With a strong, sharp knife, cut into the skin in parallel lines, 15 mm /½ in apart, going at a slant in one direction, then score the skin in the other direction, to make a pattern.
5 Lay the pork in a roasting tin. Rub the olive oil into the skin and season the whole joint generously with salt and pepper.
6 Roast the pork for 15 minutes.
7 Meanwhile, drain the soaked prunes and apricots, reserving the liquids. Stone the prunes if necessary.
8 In a bowl, mix the fruits with the coarsely chopped onion and add a generous seasoning of thyme, salt and pepper.
9 Remove the pork from the oven. Surround it with the fruit and onion mixture and dot the pork with butter.
10 Return the tin to the oven and immediately turn the temperature down to 150C /300F /gas 2.
11 Quarter, peel and core the apples and brush with a little lemon juice.
12 When the pork has been back in the oven for 15 minutes, add the apples to the roasting tin, mixing with the other fruits.
13 Continue to roast for about 45 minutes, or until the pork is tender, basting it occasionally with the reserved soaking liquid.
14 Serve the pork surrounded by the fruits. Skim the pan juices of fat, then spoon over the fruits.

 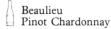 soaking, bringing to room temperature, then 1½ hours   Beaulieu Pinot Chardonnay

Individual rice moulds with sweetcorn

Serves 4

175 g /6 oz long-grain rice
salt
lemon juice
75 g /3 oz frozen sweetcorn kernels, defrosted and drained
freshly ground black pepper
melted butter, for greasing

1 Bring a large saucepan of salted water to the boil and add a squeeze of lemon juice. Dribble in the rice without letting the water come off the boil.
2 Stir once with a wooden spoon to dislodge any grains stuck to the bottom of the pan, then boil gently for 15–18 minutes, uncovered, until the rice is tender but not mushy.
3 Drain the rice, rinse it with hot water and then drain it again thoroughly.
4 Heat the oven to 150C /300F /gas 2.
5 Stir the sweetcorn into the drained rice and season to taste with salt and freshly ground black pepper.
6 Brush 4 × 150 ml /5 fl oz individual soufflé dishes or flameproof ramekins with melted butter. Spoon in the seasoned rice and sweetcorn mixture, pressing it down gently and making sure that the mixture comes level with the tops — this will stop them collapsing when they are turned out.
7 Place the dishes on a baking tray. Cover each dish with foil and cook the rice in the oven for 20 minutes.
8 Protecting your hands with oven gloves, invert each dish in turn onto a heated serving platter and give the base of the dish a little tap. Remove the dishes very carefully and serve the rice moulds immediately.

 defrosting, then 45 minutes

Steamed peas with ham fingers

Serves 4
450 g /1 lb frozen peas, defrosted
30 ml /2 tbls finely chopped spring onions or shallots
50 g /2 oz butter
1 slice of cooked ham, 5 mm /¼ in thick
15 ml /1 tbls lemon juice
salt and freshly ground black pepper

1 Place the defrosted peas in the top pan of a double boiler with the finely chopped spring onions or shallots and 25 g /1 oz of the butter. Cover and cook over boiling water for 7 minutes, or until tender.
2 Meanwhile, cut the cooked ham into 5 cm × 5 mm /2 × ¼ in strips.
3 In a small frying-pan, heat the remaining butter and sauté the ham for 4 minutes, or until it is golden, tossing it with a spatula.
4 In a heated serving dish, combine the steamed peas and spring onions or shallots with the sautéed ham strips. Flavour this to taste with lemon juice and season with salt and freshly ground black pepper. Serve as soon as possible.

defrosting the peas,
then 10 minutes

Rhubarb compote with redcurrant jelly

Serves 4
900 g /2 lb rhubarb
120 ml /8 tbls redcurrant jelly
275 ml /10 fl oz thick cream, to serve

1 Heat the oven to 180C /350F /gas 4.
2 Wipe the rhubarb with a damp cloth and trim off the ends. Cut each stick into 5 cm /2 in lengths.
3 In an ovenproof serving dish large enough to take the rhubarb batons in one layer, arrange them in neat rows. Cover them with the redcurrant jelly.
4 Cover the dish and cook for 45 minutes, or until the rhubarb batons are tender but still whole.
5 Leave the rhubarb to get cold and then serve it with a jug of thick cream.

1 hour, plus cooling

A TASTE OF PARADISE

Asparagus salad

Hawaiian pork chops

Celery and mushroom
Chinese-style

Green beans with soy sauce

Pilaff with raisins
and pine nuts

Gateau noisette

Wine: Provence rosé, or another dry rosé

One of the reasons why tender fresh asparagus is such a treat is that it is in season for a very short time — a couple of months at the most. This menu does full justice to this delicious early-summer vegetable, with the Asparagus salad starter. The delicate heads are gently steamed, then served cold on top of large sprigs of fresh fennel, together with a piquant soured cream dressing, sharpened with lemon juice and flavoured with fresh parsley, chives and tarragon. Choose your asparagus carefully — look out for crisp stalks with compact green tips, and avoid 'woody-looking' stalks and discoloured ends, which often mean that the asparagus has been travelling too long.

The main course brings your guests an extra taste of the sun with Hawaiian pork chops. The meat is cooked very simply under the grill; it is the fruit garnish which adds extra flavour, as well as transforming the chops into an extremely attractive dish. Slices of apple are glazed under the grill and then pineapple slices and grapes top the chop just before serving. To go with the succulent fruity flavours of the Hawaiian pork chops choose a crisp, fresh Chinese-style vegetable. Choose either my stir-fried Celery and mushrooms, Chinese-style , or Green beans with soy sauce. Both these dishes can be quickly prepared between the first and the main course, serving straight from the wok or frying-pan to the table. To accompany one of these two dishes Pilaff with raisins and pine nuts is a colourful dish which can be assembled quickly just before the meal and popped into the oven, ready to serve with no more attention.

The dessert, Gateau noisette, is a dinner party dream. A crisp meringue sandwiched with rich dark chocolate and hazelnut butter cream, this gateau tastes even better if cooked a day ahead and left overnight to mature. Needing absolutely no last minute attention, it leaves the host or hostess entirely free to concentrate on the other courses, and on enjoying the party.

To drink with this summery menu I have chosen a crisp, dry rosé from the Côtes de Provence in the south of France. Any other dry rosé would be suitable and a good indication of dryness is a very pale pink wine.

Plan-ahead timetable

On the day before the meal
Gateau noisette: make and cook the meringue and make the filling. Assemble the gateau and store it in a cool place.

Two hours before the meal
Asparagus salad: prepare the asparagus and dressing.
Hawaiian pork chops: prepare and bring to room temperature.
Celery and mushrooms, Chinese-style (if using): wash, dry

and cut the celery into slices. Wipe and slice the mushrooms.
Green beans with soy sauce (if using): wash, trim and cut the
beans.

Thirty minutes before the meal
Hawaiian pork chops: heat the grill. Slice the apple. Grill the
pork chops and the sugared apple slices. Keep hot.

Fifteen minutes before the meal
Pilaff with raisins and pine nuts: heat the oven. Sauté the
onion, rice and pine nuts. Prepare the stock and bake the pilaff.

Between the first and the main course
Hawaiian pork chops: grill the pineapple, garnish the chops and
serve.
Celery and mushrooms, Chinese-style (if using): stir-fry the
vegetables. Add the sauce and finish cooking. Transfer to a
heated serving dish.
Green beans with soy sauce (if using): cook the beans and make
the sauce and serve.
Pilaff with raisins and pine nuts: transfer to a serving dish; add
the raisins, pine nuts and butter.

Asparagus salad

Serves 4
1 kg /2 lb fresh asparagus
salt
12 large sprigs of fennel
**For the soured cream
dressing**
150 ml /5 fl oz soured cream
15 ml /1 tbls lemon juice
salt
freshly ground black pepper

15 ml /1 tbls finely chopped
  fresh parsley
15 ml /1 tbls finely snipped
  chives
15 ml /1 tbls finely chopped fresh
  tarragon
a dash of Tabasco or a pinch of
  paprika
5 ml /1 tsp snipped chives, to
  garnish

1 Wash the asparagus stalks well in cold water. Scrape the stems with a knife to remove the scaly leaf points. Cut off the tough woody ends and ensure that the stalks are the same length.
2 Using soft string, tie the asparagus in a bundle in two different places, just below the tips and further down the stems.
3 In a deep, narrow saucepan in which the stalks can stand upright, bring to the boil enough salted water to come halfway up the asparagus. This ensures that the tough stalks become tender while the heads cook in the steam. If your pan is not deep enough, extend the sides with foil, making them high enough to stand above the tips. If your pan is not narrow enough, stand the asparagus in a tall glass jar half-filled with boiled salted water, cover the top with foil and set in a pan of simmering water. Simmer for at least 12 minutes according to size, until the thick part of the stalk feels tender when pierced with a sharp knife.
4 Drain the asparagus and refresh under cold running water. Drain again and lay on a folded clean tea-towel to absorb any remaining water. Leave to cool.
5 In a bowl, combine the soured cream and lemon juice; season to taste. Add the herbs and a dash of Tabasco or a pinch of paprika and stir until the dressing is smooth and well-blended.
6 To serve, lay 3 sprigs of fennel on each of 4 plates with the asparagus. Spoon 30 ml /2 tbls soured cream dressing on the side of each plate and serve the remaining dressing separately, garnished with a sprinkling of snipped chives.

● You can use frozen asparagus, cooked from frozen in a small quantity of boiling salted water for 5–6 minutes, or until just tender.
● Provide a finger bowl with a thin slice of lemon floating on it and a large cloth napkin for each guest.

35–55 minutes

Hawaiian pork chops

Serves 4
4 × 175 g /6 oz pork chops, about 20 mm /¾ in thick
freshly ground black pepper
30 ml /2 tbls olive oil
salt
15–30 ml /1–2 tbls melted butter
1 dessert apple, thickly sliced
15 ml /1 tbls brown sugar
4 pineapple slices, with core removed
100 g /4 oz green grapes
4 cloves
4 bay leaves

1 Wipe the chops with absorbent paper and trim off the excess fat, leaving only a narrow layer. With a sharp knife, slash the layer of fat at regular intervals to stop the chop curling up under the heat of the grill. Season with freshly ground black pepper and leave to come to room temperature.
2 Heat the grill to high.
3 Brush the chops with the olive oil and season with salt and freshly ground black pepper. Grill the chops 7.5 cm /3 in from the heat for 6 minutes on each side, or until they are brown and tender. Transfer the chops to a heated serving platter and keep warm.
4 With a little of the melted butter, brush the apple slices and place them on a strip of foil. Lay the foil on the grid of the grill pan, sprinkle the apple slices with brown sugar and grill for 4–5 minutes on the sugared side only until golden. Keep warm.
5 Brush the pineapple slices with the remaining melted butter and place them on a strip of foil. Lay the foil on the grid of the grill pan and heat the pineapple slices through for 2 minutes on each side, turning carefully with a fish slice.
6 Arrange a pineapple slice on the top of each chop. Lay 3 slices of glazed apple next to the pineapple, and fill the hollowed-out pineapple core with grapes. Pierce a bay leaf with a clove, and attach to the pineapple. Serve immediately.

35 minutes a Provence rosé,
or another dry rosé

Celery and mushrooms, Chinese-style

Serves 4
9 sticks of celery
350 g /12 oz large mushrooms
45 ml /3 tbls peanut oil
salt and freshly ground black pepper
45 ml /3 tbls dry sherry
30 ml /2 tbls soy sauce
2.5–5 ml /½–1 tsp sugar

1 Wash and dry the celery sticks, then cut them into diagonal slices, 5 mm /¼ in thick.
2 Wipe the mushrooms with a damp cloth. With a sharp knife, trim the stalks and cut the mushrooms into 5 mm /¼ in thick slices.
3 Heat the peanut oil in a large frying-pan or wok and stir-fry the sliced celery over high heat for 3–4 minutes, tossing frequently with a fish slice, or stirring with chopsticks if you are using a wok. Add the sliced mushrooms, season to taste with salt and freshly ground black pepper. Stir-fry for a further 2 minutes. Add the dry sherry, soy sauce and sugar. Mix well with a wooden spoon and then bring to the boil.
4 Remove from the heat and transfer the vegetables to a heated serving platter. Pour the pan juices over the vegetables and serve.

 20 minutes

Green beans with soy sauce

Serves 4
450 g /1 lb green beans
45 ml /3 tbls peanut oil
5 ml /1 tsp salt
10 ml /2 tsp soy sauce
30 ml /2 tbls dry sherry

1 Wash and trim the beans. Cut them into 5 cm /2 in lengths.
2 Heat the oil in a wok or frying-pan. Add the beans and cook over a medium heat for 1 minute, stirring constantly with a spatula.
3 Add the salt and 150 ml /5 fl oz water. Cover the pan and cook the beans for 3 minutes.
4 Remove the cover and simmer gently, stirring from time to time, for 5 minutes, or until the water has evaporated.
5 Stir in the soy sauce and dry sherry.
6 Transfer to a serving dish and serve as soon as possible.

 20 minutes

Pilaff with raisins and pine nuts

Serves 4
50 g /2 oz seedless raisins
60 g /2½ oz butter
15 ml /1 tbls olive oil
½ Spanish onion, finely chopped
225 g /8 oz long-grain rice
1 chicken stock cube
salt and freshly ground black pepper
25 g /1 oz pine nuts, sautéed in butter until golden
flat-leaved parsley, to garnish

1 Cover the seedless raisins with boiling water to soak. Heat the oven to 190C /375F /gas 5.
2 Heat 40 g /1½ oz butter in a heavy flameproof casserole with the olive oil. When the foaming subsides, add the finely chopped onion and sauté for about 10 minutes, or until soft but not coloured.
3 Add the rice and stir over a moderate heat for 2–3 minutes until the grains are thoroughly coated with butter.
4 Dissolve the stock cube in 425 ml /15 fl oz boiling water in a saucepan and bring back to the boil. Pour the boiling stock into the casserole, taking care as the stock will sizzle when it comes into contact with the hot butter. Season to taste with salt and freshly ground black pepper and quickly cover the casserole to prevent too much stock from evaporating.
5 Transfer to the oven and bake the pilaff for 15–20 minutes, or until the rice grains are fluffed and separate and the liquid has been absorbed. Meanwhile, sauté the pine nuts and drain the raisins.
6 Transfer the pilaff to a serving dish, add the drained, soaked raisins, sautéed pine nuts and the remaining butter. Toss with a fork to mix them in lightly. Taste and add more salt and freshly ground black pepper, if necessary. Garnish with a little flat-leaved parsley and serve.

50 minutes

Gateau noisette

Serves 4–6
6 egg whites
350 g /12 oz caster sugar
For the crème au beurre
2 egg whites
100 g /4 oz icing sugar
225 g /8 oz unsalted butter, softened
100 g /4 oz dark cooking chocolate
5 ml /1 tsp lemon juice
150 g /5 oz hazelnuts, chopped

1 Heat the oven to 150C /300F /gas 2, arranging the shelves below the centre. Line 2 baking sheets with oiled greaseproof or non-stick silicone paper. Draw two circles on each sheet of paper, each about 15–18 cm /6–7 in in diameter.
2 In a large bowl, whisk the egg whites with a wire whisk or a rotary beater until they are light and frothy. Whisk in 50 g /2 oz of the caster sugar and continue whisking until the whites form stiff peaks. With a metal spoon, carefully fold in the remaining sugar.
3 Using a piping bag fitted with a 10 mm /½ in plain nozzle, pipe the meringue mixture around each of the circles, starting just inside the guideline and working inwards in a spiral to make a circle. Bake for about 1 hour. Turn the meringue circles over, still attached to the paper, and bake for a further 15 minutes. Remove the meringue circles from the oven and leave to cool.
4 For the filling choose a bowl which firmly fits over a large saucepan. Pour 5 cm /2 in of water into the pan and bring to the boil. Reduce to a gentle simmer, set the bowl over the saucepan and combine the egg whites with the icing sugar in the bowl. Whisk continually, preferably with a hand-held electric beater, over barely simmering water until the mixture thickens and is stiff and mousse-like — about 4 minutes. Remove the bowl from the heat.
5 In a second bowl, cream the butter until it is light and fluffy. Gradually add the cooked mousse to the butter, beating well.
6 In the top pan of a double boiler, melt the chocolate over low heat. As soon as the chocolate has melted, remove the pan from the heat. Beat the melted chocolate into the butter mixture, then add the lemon juice and half the chopped hazelnuts, beating well.
7 Remove the cold meringue circles from the paper. Put one meringue layer on a flat serving plate. Spread about 1/5 of the chocolate filling over the meringue circle, then gently place another circle on top and spread some more filling over it. Repeat with the remaining meringue circles and filling, covering the top of the gateau with chocolate filling. Top with the remaining hazelnuts.
8 Leave the gateau in a refrigerator or a cool place for about 24 hours before serving.

 1¾ hours, then 24 hours maturing

Fish

MEDITERRANEAN CUISINE

Tagliatelle with tomato and basil sauce

Sardines stuffed with spinach

Grapefruit mint salad

Cherries jubilee

Wine: Vinho Verde

Plan-ahead timetable

On the morning of the meal
Tagliatelle with tomato and basil sauce: make the sauce but do not add the butter or cheese. Reserve.
Cherries jubilee: prepare and cook the cherries, make the sauce and reserve both until needed.

One hour before the meal
Cherries jubilee: transfer the vanilla ice cream to the main part of the refrigerator.
Grapefruit mint salad: wash, dry and chill the lettuces. Prepare the grapefruit. Make the dressing.

This menu for six will transport your guests to all parts of the Mediterranean. For the first course I have chosen an Italian pasta dish of tagliatelle coated with a delicious summery sauce of tomato and fresh basil. Rich with dry white wine, butter and freshly grated Parmesan cheese, it is a smooth, tempting dish redolent of sun-warmed hillsides and long evenings. If at all possible, buy your tagliatelle fresh from an Italian delicatessen — I think freshly made pasta has a superb flavour, which is quite different from that of dry pasta. Fresh tagliatelle can now be bought vacuum-packed from many supermarkets.

The main course is reminiscent of holidays by the sea in the sunny South of France, where juicy sardines, fresh and sparkling, are taken straight from the sea and grilled whole over charcoal. Our own imported sardines, with that first gloss of freshness lost during the journey, are definitely better cleaned — for ease, ask your fishmonger to do this for you. Serve the sardines baked with an elegant spinach stuffing, with a hint of garlic and onion for extra flavour. To go with them I have chosen a sharp, fresh-tasting Grapefruit mint salad — an unusual combination of lettuce and grapefruit with a lemony, mint dressing.

To finish the meal, use lovely seasonal fruit to make Cherries jubilee. A delightful combination of ripe, sweet black cherries in a hot brandy sauce with velvety smooth vanilla ice cream, it is also easy to make and a perfect dessert for a summer dinner party. (If you wish to make this dessert when cherries are not in season — and their season is short — frozen, bottled or canned ones can be used instead. It is more convenient to buy cans of stoned rather than unstoned cherries and remember, inside a 425 g /15 oz can of stoned cherries there will be 225 g /8 oz of drained fruit.) Conveniently, you can prepare the cherries ahead, and only have to flame the brandy quickly and gently heat through the cherry sauce and the cherries at the last minute.

Thirty minutes before the meal

Sardines stuffed with spinach: prepare and sauté the spinach, garlic and onion. Season and spread ⅔ of the mixture in the gratin dish.

Fifteen minutes before the meal

Tagliatelle with basil and tomato sauce: add the butter, grated Parmesan cheese and seasoning to the sauce and heat gently. Cook the tagliatelle.
Sardines stuffed with spinach: heat the oven.

Just before the meal

Tagliatelle with tomato and basil sauce: drain the pasta and toss in a serving bowl with the butter, grated Parmesan cheese and the basil and tomato sauce.
Sardines stuffed with spinach: stuff and roll the sardines; place them on the vegetable mixture in the gratin dish and bake.

Between the first and the main course

Grapefruit mint salad: combine the salad ingredients. Toss with the dressing, add the grapefruit segments and garnish.

Between the main course and the dessert

Cherries jubilee: heat the cherries and the sauce. Divide the vanilla ice cream into portions. Flambé the brandy and cherry brandy sauce and pour over the vanilla ice cream.

Tagliatelle with tomato and basil sauce

Serves 6

500 g /1 lb tagliatelle
salt
75 g /3 oz butter
90 ml /6 tbls freshly grated
    Parmesan cheese
16 fresh basil leaves, shredded,
    or 15 ml /1 tbls dried basil
For the tomato and basil sauce
1½ Spanish onions
3 garlic cloves
3 medium-sized carrots

2 celery sticks
900 g /2 lb ripe tomatoes
400 g /14 oz canned peeled
    tomatoes
200 ml /7 fl oz dry white wine
16 fresh basil leaves, shredded, or
    15 ml /1 tbls dried basil
75 g /3 oz butter
90 ml /6 tbls freshly grated
    Parmesan cheese
salt
freshly ground black pepper

1 First prepare the tomato and basil sauce. Finely chop the onions, garlic, carrots and celery and place them in a large saucepan.
2 Coarsely chop the ripe tomatoes and add them to the saucepan, along with the canned peeled tomatoes and their juice, the dry white wine and shredded fresh basil or dried basil. Stir well. Bring to the boil, then lower the heat and simmer, covered, for 1 hour, until the vegetables are tender.
3 Pass the sauce through a sieve, pressing the vegetables through with the back of a wooden spoon. The sauce should be fairly thick; if it is too thin, return it to a saucepan and simmer, uncovered, until it is the desired consistency.
4 Add the butter to the sauce, the freshly grated Parmesan cheese and salt and pepper to taste. Stir the sauce over a gentle heat until it is hot, and the butter has melted. Keep warm.
5 Bring a 4.5 L /8 pt saucepan of salted water to the boil and cook the tagliatelle until it is tender but still firm. Stir occasionally with a fork to keep the strands separate.
6 Thoroughly drain the cooked tagliatelle in a colander and heap it into a heated serving bowl. Add the butter, freshly grated Parmesan cheese and shredded fresh basil or dried basil. Toss with a serving fork and spoon. Pour the hot tomato and basil sauce over the tagliatelle and toss vigorously with the fork and spoon until the strands are thoroughly coated with the sauce. Serve immediately.

 1½ hours

Sardines stuffed with spinach

Serves 6

18 fresh sardines (about 1.4 kg /3 lb), cleaned with the heads,
    fins and backbones removed
1.4 kg /3 lb fresh spinach
120 ml /8 tbls olive oil
2 garlic cloves
1 Spanish onion, finely chopped
salt and freshly ground black pepper
freshly grated nutmeg
30 ml /2 tbls toasted breadcrumbs
To serve
crusty French bread

1 Heat the oven to 190C /375F /gas 5.
2 Remove the stems from the spinach and wash the leaves carefully several times in cold water, discarding any damaged leaves. Drain the spinach well.
3 Heat 30 ml /2 tbls of the olive oil in a large saucepan and add as much of the spinach as the pan will hold. Cook until the leaves become limp and reduce in volume, then add more spinach. Continue until all the spinach is in the pan. Cook until the leaves are limp.
4 Squeeze out the excess liquid from the cooked spinach leaves and chop them finely, together with the garlic cloves.
5 Heat 60 ml /4 tbls of the remaining olive oil in a frying-pan and sauté the finely chopped onion until golden. Add the finely chopped spinach and garlic, and season to taste with salt, freshly ground pepper and freshly grated nutmeg. Mix the ingredients well. Spread ⅔ of the spinach and onion mixture in the bottom of a gratin dish.
6 Place the prepared sardines, open side up, on absorbent paper. Place 15 ml /1 tbls of the remaining spinach and onion mixture on each sardine. Roll the fish up tightly from the head end. Place them in rows on the bed of spinach.
7 Sprinkle the sardines with the toasted breadcrumbs and then with the remaining olive oil. Bake the sardines in the oven for about 20 minutes. Serve immediately with crusty French bread.

● Frozen sardines can also be used for this dish.

 1 hour   Vinho Verde

Grapefruit mint salad

Serves 6
½ round lettuce
½ cos lettuce
1 grapefruit
5–10 ml /1–2 tsp lemon juice
90 ml /6 tbls olive oil
salt and freshly ground black pepper
20 fresh mint leaves, finely chopped
For the garnish
6 fresh mint leaves

1 Wash the lettuces carefully. Pat the leaves dry with a clean tea-towel and chill them, rolled up in a clean cloth, in the salad drawer of the refrigerator until needed.
2 Peel the grapefruit with a sharp knife, slicing off the pith and membrane, together with the skin, and catching the juice in a small bowl. Cut down on each side of the segments and lift them out of the membranes.
3 Combine the grapefruit juice with the lemon juice and the olive oil, beating with a fork until the mixture emulsifies. Season it with salt and freshly ground black pepper to taste and then stir in the finely chopped fresh mint leaves.
4 Just before serving, tear the chilled lettuce leaves into pieces and put them in a salad bowl. Pour the emulsified dressing over it and toss thoroughly until all the leaves are well coated. Finally add the grapefruit segments, toss the salad again, garnish it with the fresh mint leaves and serve immediately.

20 minutes

Cherries jubilee

Serves 6
1.1 L /2 pt vanilla ice cream
700 g /1½ lb ripe, sweet black cherries
45 ml /3 tbls caster sugar
7.5 cm /3 in cinnamon stick
finely grated zest and juice of 1 orange
7.5 ml /1½ tsp cornflour
60–75 ml /4–5 tbls brandy
60–75 ml /4–5 tbls cherry brandy

1 About 1 hour before you intend to serve the dessert, transfer the vanilla ice cream to the main part of the refrigerator.
2 Wash the cherries and remove the stalks and stones.
3 Combine the cherries with 350 ml /12 fl oz water in a saucepan. Simmer them for 5–10 minutes, depending on ripeness, until they are soft but not disintegrating. Transfer the cherries to a bowl, using a slotted spoon. Reserve the juices.
4 Add the caster sugar, cinnamon stick and finely grated zest and juice of the orange to the juices remaining in the pan.
5 In a small bowl, mix the cornflour to a smooth paste with 15 ml / 1 tbls of the liquid from the pan. Stir this into the liquid in the pan with a wooden spoon and bring the mixture to the boil. Reduce it to a simmer and cook, stirring occasionally, for 3–5 minutes, or until the liquid is a light, syrupy consistency.
6 Add the cherries to the pan and gently heat them through. Pour the contents of the pan into a wide, shallow bowl.
7 Divide the ice cream into 6 individual portions.
8 Pour the brandy and cherry brandy into a large metal ladle and hold it over an open flame, swirling it around to warm the alcohol. Set it alight with a match and, as soon as it flames, pour it over the hot cherries.
9 As soon as the flames die down, spoon the cherries jubilee over the individual portions of ice cream and serve immediately.

35 minutes

SIMPLE TO PREPARE

Classic American soup with a French name — Crème vichyssoise — was created by Louis Diat in 1910 when he was chef at the Ritz Carlton in New York. It is a purée of leeks and potatoes lightly spiced with nutmeg and cayenne pepper and blended to velvety smoothness with thick cream. Serve it chilled, garnished with chives for a truly elegant presentation.

The main course is Baked fish, Spanish-style. Made with fresh fillets of cod, hake or halibut, the fish is baked in a rich tomato sauce with white wine, olives and capers. The sauce can be made ahead and the fish will need very little attention. You can serve this dish with well-flavoured Brown rice with green pepper, and crisp Sautéed cauliflower. Don't overcook the cauliflower — it should be crunchy to contrast with the richness of the sauce in the main dish. Serve a white Rioja as the wine to match the Spanish baked fish.

Like much of this menu, the dessert can be made well in advance and will not involve you in any last minute preparations. For the summery Fresh raspberry flan, make a smooth, kirsch-flavoured custard cream to fill the pastry case and top it with fresh raspberries in a pretty redcurrant and kirsch glaze. Leave the flan to chill in the refrigerator until you are ready to enjoy it with your guests.

Crème vichyssoise

Baked fish, Spanish-style

Sautéed cauliflower

Brown rice with green pepper

Fresh raspberry flan

Wine: a white Rioja

Plan-ahead timetable

On the day before the meal
Fresh raspberry flan: make and bake the pastry case. Keep it in an airtight container.

On the morning of the meal
Fresh raspberry flan: prepare the filling and the glaze. Assemble the flan and chill.
Crème vichyssoise: make the soup and refrigerate.
Baked fish, Spanish-style: make and chill the tomato sauce.

One hour before the meal
Sautéed cauliflower: cut the cauliflower into florets, blanch and refresh. Drain.
Brown rice with green pepper: boil the rice, drain thoroughly and keep hot.
Baked fish, Spanish-style: heat the oven.

Thirty minutes before the meal
Baked fish, Spanish-style: skin the fish, prepare the gratin dish, cover and bake.
Brown rice with green pepper: cook the pepper and onion; keep warm.

Just before the first course
Crème vichyssoise: stir in the cream, pour into cups or bowls, sprinkle with chives and serve.
Baked fish, Spanish-style: remove the cover and finish baking.

Between the first and the main course
Baked fish, Spanish-style: remove from the oven, sprinkle with parsley and serve.
Sautéed cauliflower: sauté the florets, season, garnish and serve.
Brown rice with green pepper: add the vegetables to the rice, adjust the seasoning and serve.

Crème vichyssoise

Serves 4–6
50–75 g /2–3 oz butter
4 leeks, white part only, sliced
2 medium-sized onions, sliced
2 celery sticks, sliced
4 potatoes, peeled and sliced
1.1 L /2 pt chicken stock, home-made or from a cube
salt and freshly ground black pepper
a pinch of freshly grated nutmeg
a pinch of cayenne pepper
425 ml /15 fl oz thick cream, chilled
60 ml /4 tbls coarsely snipped chives

1 In a large saucepan melt the butter and sauté the sliced leeks, onions and celery until the vegetables are soft but not coloured — about 8–10 minutes.
2 Add the potatoes and chicken stock to the pan and simmer for about 30 minutes until tender.
3 Arrange a large sieve over a bowl and press the vegetables through with a wooden spoon. Alternatively, purée the soup in a blender. Season generously with salt and freshly ground black pepper, a pinch of freshly grated nutmeg and a hint of cayenne pepper. Cool, then chill the soup.
4 Just before serving, stir in the chilled thick cream and spoon the soup into chilled soup cups or bowls. Sprinkle with coarsely snipped chives.

● Crème vichyssoise is one of America's famous soups. The chef who invented it, Louis Diat, named it after the French town of Vichy, which is close to where he was born.

 45 minutes, plus chilling

Baked fish, Spanish-style

Serves 4
700 g /1½ lb cod, hake or halibut fillet
salt and freshly ground black pepper
butter, for greasing
30 ml /2 tbls finely chopped fresh parsley, to garnish
For the tomato sauce
30 ml /2 tbls olive oil
1 Spanish onion, finely chopped
400 g /14 oz canned peeled tomatoes, and their juice
150 ml /5 fl oz dry white wine
2 cloves
salt and freshly ground black pepper
15 ml /1 tbls cornflour
12 green olives, stoned and chopped
15 ml /1 tbls finely chopped fresh parsley
30 ml /2 tbls drained capers

1 Make the tomato sauce: heat the olive oil in a heavy-based saucepan. Add the finely chopped onion and cook over a moderate heat for 7 minutes, or until soft, stirring occasionally with a wooden spoon.
2 Stir in the tomatoes and their juice, the dry white wine and the cloves. Season to taste with salt and freshly ground black pepper. Cover and simmer for 20 minutes, stirring occasionally.
3 Heat the oven to 190C /375F /gas 5.
4 Blend the cornflour with a little cold water to form a smooth paste. Stir it into the tomato mixture and simmer for 1 minute. Add the chopped olives, finely chopped parsley and drained capers. Adjust the seasoning.
5 Skin the fish and cut into portions, if necessary. Season with salt and freshly ground black pepper.
6 Butter a gratin dish large enough to take the fish in one layer. Lay the fish pieces side by side in the dish and pour the tomato sauce over. Cover and bake in the oven for 20 minutes. Remove the cover and bake for a further 10 minutes, or until the fish flakes easily with a fork. Sprinkle with finely chopped parsley and serve immediately.

 1¼ hours   a white Rioja

Brown rice with green pepper

Serves 4
225 g /8 oz brown rice
salt
25 g /1 oz butter
15 ml /1 tbls olive oil
1 green pepper, cored, seeded and diced
1 medium-sized onion, finely chopped
freshly ground black pepper

1 In a large saucepan bring at least 2.3 L /4 pt salted water to the boil. When it bubbles vigorously, dribble in the rice gradually through your fingers so that the water does not stop boiling. Stir once to dislodge any grains stuck to the bottom or the sides of the pan.
2 Boil the rice for 30–35 minutes, or until it is tender but still firm to the bite.
3 While the rice is cooking, heat the butter and olive oil in a saucepan. When the foaming subsides, add the diced pepper and finely chopped onion and cook over a moderate heat for 10 minutes, or until soft, stirring with a wooden spoon. Season with salt and freshly ground black pepper to taste. Keep warm.
4 Drain the rice in a sieve and rinse thoroughly with hot water. Shake out all excess moisture and return the rice to the saucepan.
5 Toss the vegetables in the cooked rice and carefully adjust the seasoning. Transfer to a heated serving dish and serve immediately.

● Brown rice has a heavier texture than white rice and takes a lot longer to cook but its nutty wholesome flavour makes it pleasantly different.

45 minutes

Sautéed cauliflower

Serves 4
1 medium-sized cauliflower
salt
25 g /1 oz butter
15 ml /1 tbls olive oil
freshly ground black pepper
10 ml /2 tsp lemon juice

1 Cut the cauliflower into florets, then cut each floret into quarters. Bring a saucepan of salted water to the boil, add the cauliflower and blanch for 1 minute only. If cooked any longer, the water content will stop the florets from browning in the frying-pan. Drain, rinse under running cold water and drain again.
2 In a large frying-pan, heat the butter and olive oil. When the foaming subsides, add the drained cauliflower and sauté over a moderate heat for 3–4 minutes or until barely tender, tossing the florets with a spatula.
3 Season with salt and freshly ground black pepper to taste, sprinkle with lemon juice and transfer the sautéed cauliflower to a serving dish and serve immediately.

Fresh raspberry flan

Serves 4
20 cm /8 in pastry case, fully baked blind
2 egg yolks
60 ml /4 tbls icing sugar
5 ml /1 tsp cornflour
275 ml /10 fl oz milk
22.5 ml /1½ tbls kirsch
15 g /½ oz powdered gelatine
50 ml /2 fl oz thick cream, lightly whipped
700 g /1½ lb raspberries
45 ml /3 tbls redcurrant jelly
thick cream, to serve

1 In the top pan of a double boiler combine the egg yolks, icing sugar and cornflour and mix to a smooth paste with a wooden spoon.
2 Bring the milk to the boil and pour onto the egg yolk mixture, stirring all the time. Place the egg yolk mixture over simmering water and cook for 15–20 minutes, whisking continuously, until the custard thickens. Flavour it with 7.5 ml /½ tbls of kirsch and leave to cool.
3 In a small bowl, sprinkle the powdered gelatine over 45 ml /3 tbls water. Leave for a few minutes to soften. Place the bowl over the saucepan of simmering water until the gelatine dissolves. Stir the gelatine into the cooled custard.
4 Stand the bowl of custard in a bowl of crushed ice and stir occasionally as it chills to prevent a skin from forming.
5 When the custard is on the point of setting, fold in the whipped cream with a large metal spoon. Pour it into the baked pastry case and chill until set.
6 Cover the set custard with the raspberries, arranging them side by side standing upright.
7 Put the redcurrant jelly and the remaining 15 ml /1 tbls kirsch in a small saucepan and bring to a simmer. Beat with a wooden spoon until smooth. Leave to cool until tepid, then brush the mixture over the raspberries to glaze. Chill the flan before serving it accompanied by thick cream.

15–20 minutes

 making the pastry case,
1 hour, plus cooling and chilling

A DINNER FOR FISH FANS

Three miniature quiches

Sea bass with fennel
Lemon rice with pine nuts
Baked spinach mornay
Green salad with bacon dressing

Italian chestnut charlotte

Wine: St Véran or another white burgundy

An appetizer, by its very name, should tempt the appetite and not destroy it. In fact, it should be a teaser — something to whet the appetite for what is to follow. The Three miniature quiches are guaranteed to do just that — three tempting bites with three delicious flavours. And yet this unusual starter is so easy to prepare. The pastry cases can be baked in advance and the three quiche mixes assembled on the day of the party itself. Then all you have to do is pop them into the oven minutes before you are ready to sit down to dinner. There's a small added bonus, too — each of the three quiche recipes makes up to 10 individual tarts if your tart tins are the normal size (6.5 cm /2½ in in diameter, about 2 cm /¾ in deep, with sloping, unfluted sides) so you will have a few left over to serve with drinks or as a snack on another day.

The main course of this impressive dinner party for eight is a majestic Sea bass with fennel, using fennel seeds and dried fennel stalks. These are flamed with Pernod for a real South of France flavour or, if you find it more convenient, with cognac. If you see a sea bass in a fish shop but are only planning a dinner party for four, serve the great fish as it is for maximum effect and save half of the fish for later. Use this to make an instant salad the next day — very convenient for weekend guests! Toss the cubed fish, complete with the fennel seeds with which it was cooked, in a well-flavoured vinaigrette dressing.

I like to accompany the sea bass with a simple Lemon rice with pine nuts, and Baked spinach mornay. Follow this with a refreshing Green salad with bacon dressing.

For dessert, my choice is Italian chestnut charlotte; smooth, bold and delightful, it can be prepared well ahead and decorated just before your guests arrive.

My suggestion for a wine to drink with the splendid main course of Sea bass with fennel is St Véran or another white burgundy which will complement the flavours of the menu splendidly.

Plan-ahead timetable

On the day before or early on the day
Italian chestnut charlotte: make and refrigerate.
Three miniature quiches: make the pastry and bake the cases, then keep them in an airtight tin.

Two and a half hours before the meal
Sea bass with fennel: marinate the seeds in the Pernod mixture.
Green salad with bacon dressing: prepare lettuce. Make dressing.

Two hours before the meal
Sea bass with fennel: season the fish and fill the belly cavity.
Place on the fennel stalks, sprinkle with olive oil and marinate.
Baked spinach mornay: prepare the spinach, cook and reserve.
Make the mornay sauce and reserve.

One and a half hours before the meal
Italian chestnut charlotte: decorate and return to the refrigerator.
Three miniature quiches: prepare the three fillings and reserve.

Forty-five minutes before the meal
Sea bass with fennel: heat the grill or oven. Sear the fish and lay it on the fennel stalks.
Lemon rice with pine nuts: prepare the rice and onion mixture.

Thirty-five minutes before the meal
Sea bass with fennel: place the fish under the grill or in the oven.

Twenty-five minutes before the meal
Lemon rice with pine nuts: finish cooking the rice and place in the bottom of the oven to keep warm.
Three miniature quiches: add the fillings and bake.

Twenty minutes before the meal
Baked spinach mornay: reheat the mornay sauce and spinach.

Fifteen minutes before the meal
Sea bass with fennel: cover the fish with the remaining stalks of fennel and continue cooking.
Green salad with bacon dressing: tear the lettuce leaves and return them to the refrigerator.
Lemon rice with pine nuts: sauté the pine nuts; add to rice. Keep it warm in the bottom of the oven.
Baked spinach mornay: combine the spinach and sauce and grill.
Sea bass with fennel: put the fish on a platter and keep it warm.

Between the first and the main course
Green salad with bacon dressing: toss the lettuce in the dressing.
Sea bass with fennel: set the fennel stalks alight. Serve sauce.

Three miniature quiches

Serves 8

24–30 × 6 cm /2½ in baked pastry cases

For the spinach filling
25 g /1 oz butter
100 g /4 oz chopped frozen spinach, defrosted
salt and ground black pepper
100 g /4 oz cottage cheese
1 medium-sized egg, lightly beaten
1 egg yolk, lightly beaten
60 ml /4 tbls grated Parmesan
45 ml /3 tbls thick cream
a pinch of grated nutmeg

For Roquefort cream filling
75 g /3 oz Philadelphia cheese
40 g /1½ oz Roquefort cheese
30 ml /2 tbls softened butter

1 medium-sized egg, well beaten
1 egg yolk, well beaten
150 ml /5 fl oz thin cream
15 ml /1 tbls melted butter
15 ml /1 tbls chopped parsley
5 ml /1 tsp finely chopped chives
freshly ground black pepper

For prawn and bacon filling
50 g /2 oz peeled prawns
3 bacon rashers
15 g /½ oz butter
45 ml /3 tbls chopped onion
15–30 ml /1–2 tbls chopped fresh parsley
1 medium-sized egg, lightly beaten
1 egg yolk, lightly beaten
150 ml /5 fl oz thin cream
salt and ground black pepper

1 Heat the oven to 180C /350F /gas 4.
2 To prepare the spinach mixture, melt the butter and add the spinach. Cook over a low heat for 10 minutes, then season to taste. Drain the spinach and then purée in a blender with the cottage cheese, egg and egg yolk, Parmesan cheese, cream and nutmeg.
3 To prepare the Roquefort cream mixture, mix the Philadelphia cheese with the Roquefort and softened butter in a bowl, with a wooden spoon, until smooth. Add the well-beaten egg and egg yolk, thin cream and melted butter and blend thoroughly. Press the mixture through a sieve. Stir in the finely chopped herbs and season.
4 To prepare the prawn and bacon mixture, chop the prawns. Sauté the bacon in the butter until crisp, then remove from the pan. Add the finely chopped onion to the same pan and sauté until transparent. Drain on absorbent paper. Finely chop the bacon and combine with the prawns, onion and parsley. Spoon the mixture into 8 or 10 pastry cases. Combine the lightly beaten egg and egg yolk with the thin cream and seasoning. Pour this into the cases.
5 Divide the spinach and cheese fillings among the remaining pastry cases and bake for 15 minutes.

 making the pastry cases, then 45 minutes

Sea bass with fennel

Serves 8

1.6–1.8 kg /3½–4 lb sea bass
30 ml /2 tbls fennel seeds
60 ml /4 tbls Pernod or Ricard
30 ml /2 tbls lemon juice

salt and black pepper
250 g /8 oz dried fennel stalks
150 ml /5 fl oz olive oil
2 lemons, cut in quarters, to garnish

1 Ask the fishmonger to scale, remove the guts and clean the bass for you. Wash the fish under cold running water and dry carefully, both inside and out, with a cloth or absorbent paper.
2 Put the fennel seeds in a small bowl, add the Pernod or Ricard and lemon juice and marinate the seeds in this mixture for 30 minutes.
3 Season the fish generously inside and out with salt and black pepper. Spoon the fennel seed mixture into the belly cavity.
4 Arrange a bed of half the fennel stalks on a dish large enough to hold the fish and sprinkle over 60 ml /4 tbls of the olive oil. Lay the fish on top and cover with the remaining fennel stalks. Sprinkle with 60 ml /4 tbls olive oil and marinate for at least 1 hour.
5 Heat the grill to high for 20 minutes before cooking the fish. If your grill is too small, heat the oven to 220C /425F /gas 7. Brush the grid of the grill pan with a little of the olive oil (or oil a baking tray large enough to take the fish).
6 Carefully heat a poker or thick skewer until red hot. Remove the fennel stalks covering the fish and transfer them to the grid of the grill pan or baking tray. Sear the uppermost side of the fish in a lattice pattern with the hot poker or skewer.
7 Place the fish on the fennel stalks in the grill pan or baking tray, add salt and freshly ground black pepper to taste, and pour the remaining olive oil over it, and any oil left from the fennel marinade. Reserve the remaining fennel stalks.
8 Grill or bake the fish for 20 minutes, basting frequently with the cooking juices, then cover with the remaining fennel stalks and continue to grill or bake until the fish is cooked through. This will take about 8–10 minutes longer, depending on its size and thickness. To test the fish is cooked, make a small slit and check that the flesh is opaque.
9 When ready to serve, arrange the fennel stalks on a warmed, heatproof serving dish large enough to hold the fish comfortably. Lay the bass on top and garnish with lemon quarters. Set the fennel stalks alight and serve carefully before the flames die out.

● Serve with hollandaise or fresh tomato sauce.

 1½ hours marinating, plus 45 minutes

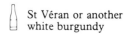 St Véran or another white burgundy

Lemon rice with pine nuts

Serves 8
550 g /1¼ lb long-grain rice
1 Spanish onion, finely chopped
50 g /2 oz butter
600 ml /1 pt well-flavoured hot chicken stock, home-made or from
*   a cube*
1 thin strip lemon zest
1.5 ml /¼ tsp dried thyme
salt and freshly ground black pepper
juice of ½ lemon
60 ml /4 tbls pine nuts

1   Heat the oven to 180C /350F /gas 4. Wash the rice under cold running water, then drain.
2   In a flameproof casserole dish or ovenproof pan, sauté the finely chopped onion in 40 g /1½ oz of the butter for about 10 minutes until a light golden colour.
3   Add the rice and continue to cook for about 5 minutes, stirring constantly, until the rice begins to colour.
4   Pour in the chicken stock and season with the strip of lemon zest, thyme, salt and freshly ground black pepper to taste.
5   Cover and place in the oven for 12–20 minutes, or until the liquid has been absorbed and the rice is tender but still firm and not mushy. Add the lemon juice and toss gently. Remove the lemon strip.
6   Melt the remaining butter, add the pine nuts and toss for a few minutes until pale golden. Spoon the rice into a heated serving dish, if wished, and garnish with the pine nuts.

● Pine nuts are the kernels of the stone pine, *Pinus pinea*. They are used in the cooking of Middle Eastern and Mediterranean countries — Lebanon and Italy in particular. They are expensive but blanched almonds can be used as a cheaper substitute.

○ 45 minutes

Baked spinach mornay

Serves 8
900 g /2 lb frozen spinach, thawed
150 g /5 oz butter
salt and freshly ground black pepper
120 ml /8 tbls thick cream
For the mornay sauce
25 g /1 oz butter
30 ml /2 tbls flour
275 ml /10 fl oz milk, warmed
60–90 ml /4–6 tbls thick cream
2.5 ml /½ tsp mustard powder
90 ml /6 tbls freshly grated black pepper
a pinch of cayenne pepper

1   Grease a shallow flameproof dish. Place the thawed spinach in a heavy-based saucepan with 50 g /2 oz butter and salt and pepper to taste. Set the pan over a low heat and cook the spinach gently for 3–6 minutes, stirring occasionally.
2   Remove the pan from the heat and stir in the cream. Turn the creamy spinach mixture into the prepared gratin dish and keep warm.
3   Prepare the mornay sauce. In a small heavy-based saucepan, melt the butter over a low heat. Remove from the heat and stir in the flour. Return the pan to a low heat and cook, stirring continuously, for 1–2 minutes until the roux is thick and smooth, but not coloured.
4   Remove the pan from the heat and add the warmed milk gradually, stirring vigorously. Return the pan to a low heat and cook, stirring, until the sauce begins to thicken. Stir in the cream, mustard and 75 ml /5 tbls grated cheese. Add salt and black pepper to taste and a pinch of cayenne, then simmer the sauce gently for a further 5 minutes. Meanwhile, heat the grill to high.
5   Pour the mornay sauce over the spinach and sprinkle the surface with the remaining cheese. Dot the remaining butter over the cheese, then place the dish under the grill for 1–2 minutes until the top is bubbling and golden brown.

○ 35 minutes

Green salad with bacon dressing

Serves 8

2–3 heads of lettuce, according to size
120–135 ml /8–9 tbls olive oil
30–45 ml /2–3 tbls wine vinegar or lemon juice
30–45 ml /2–3 tbls thick cream
2 hard-boiled eggs, finely chopped
2 bacon slices, grilled and crumbled
freshly ground black pepper
a dash of Tabasco

1 Wash the lettuce leaves carefully. Shake them dry in a salad basket or pat each leaf dry individually using absorbent paper or a cloth. Wrap in a clean cloth and leave to crisp in the bottom of the refrigerator until ready to use.
2 To make the dressing, combine the olive oil, wine vinegar or lemon juice and thick cream in a small bowl and whisk until smooth. Stir in the finely chopped hard-boiled eggs and crumbled bacon, and season to taste with freshly ground black pepper and a dash of Tabasco.
3 Just before serving, tear the lettuce leaves coarsely into a salad bowl. Pour the dressing over the salad, toss thoroughly and serve.

15 minutes, plus crisping time

Italian chestnut charlotte

Serves 8

butter, for greasing
60 ml /4 tbls dark rum
32 sponge fingers
600 ml /1 pt thick cream
60 ml /4 tbls caster sugar
225 g /8 oz unsweetened chestnut purée
7.5 g /¼ oz powdered gelatine
For the decoration
150 ml /5 fl oz thick cream
marrons glacés

1 Lightly butter a 1.7 L /3 pt charlotte mould and cut a round of greaseproof paper to fit the base. Butter the round of paper.
2 Mix the rum with 60 ml /4 tbls water in a shallow saucer.
3 Measure the sponge fingers against the side of the charlotte mould and note how much they project. Cut the tips off enough fingers to line the sides of the mould, and then dip their backs in the rum and water mixture. Line the mould sides with the sponge fingers, sugar side to the mould and the cut end to the base.
4 Arrange 4 fingers in a cross on the base of the mould inside the ring of fingers, noting where to cut each one to a point so that they fit together neatly. Cut the fingers, then dip the back of each one in the rum mixture. Arrange them in the base of the mould, sugar side down. Cut and dip more fingers in the same way to line the mould in a star shape.
5 In a bowl, combine 150 ml /5 fl oz thick cream with the caster sugar and chestnut purée. Mix to a smooth paste.
6 In a small bowl, sprinkle the gelatine over 30 ml /2 tbls cold water and leave to soften. Place the bowl in a saucepan of simmering water and leave until the gelatine is dissolved. Stir, then leave to cool.
7 Whip the remaining cream until stiff peaks form. Using a whisk, mix the gelatine into the chestnut mixture, then fold in the whipped cream.
8 Fill the prepared charlotte mould with the mixture and transfer it to the refrigerator for 3–4 hours until it is set.
9 To serve the charlotte, turn it out and remove the greaseproof paper.
10 Whip the cream and then pipe a scalloped line around the top and bottom edges of the charlotte, and a rosette in the centre.
11 Slice the marrons glacés and arrange them on the cream. Keep chilled until ready to serve.

 1 hour,
plus chilling and decorating